THINKING THROUGH SOURCES

for

Ways of the World

A Brief Global History

VOLUME 2: SINCE THE FIFTEENTH CENTURY

ROBERT W. STRAYER

The College at Brockport: State University of New York

ERIC W. NELSON

Missouri State University

THIRD EDITION

bedford/st.martin's
Macmillan Learning
Boston | New York

For Evelyn Rhiannon with Love

For Bedford/St. Martin's

Vice President, Editorial, Macmillan Learning Humanities: Edwin Hill
Publisher for History: Michael Rosenberg
Acquiring Editor for History: Laura Arcari
Director of Development for History: Jane Knetzger
Senior Developmental Editor: Leah R. Strauss
Senior Production Editor: Christina M. Horn
Assistant Production Editor: Erica Zhang
Production Manager: Joe Ford
Executive Marketing Manager: Sandra McGuire
Copy Editor: Jennifer Brett Greenstein
Photo Researcher: Bruce Carson

Director of Rights and Permissions: Hilary Newman
Senior Art Director: Anna Palchik
Text Design: Joyce Weston
Cover Design: William Boardman
Cover Photos: top, Mozambique, Maputo. *The Tree of Life*, 2005. Photograph © David Rose/Panos Pictures; bottom, Ritual of the whirling dervishes at Konya (vellum), Ottoman School, (17th century)/Private Collection/Bridgeman Images
Composition: Jouve
Printing and Binding: RR Donnelley

Manufactured in the United States of America.

1 0 9 8 7 6
f   e   d   c   b

For information, write: Bedford/St. Martin's, 75 Arlington Street, Boston, MA 02116
(617-399-4000)

ISBN 978-1-319-07464-7 (Volume 1)
ISBN 978-1-319-07465-4 (Volume 2)

Preface

Designed specifically to be used with all versions of *Ways of the World*, Third Edition, this document collection complements and extends each chapter of the parent textbook. As the title of the collection suggests, these document projects enable students to "**think through sources**" and thus begin to understand the craft of historians as well as their conclusions. They explore in greater depth a central theme from each chapter, and they integrate both documentary and visual sources. Each source includes a brief headnote that provides context for the source and several questions to consider, and the chapter ends with a series of probing essay questions appropriate for in-class discussion and writing assignments.

In addition to this print volume, we are delighted to offer the **Thinking through Sources document projects** in LaunchPad, Bedford's learning platform. In LaunchPad, these features are surrounded by a distinctive and sophisticated pedagogy of auto-graded exercises. Featuring immediate substantive feedback for each rejoinder, these exercises help students learn even when they select the wrong answer. These unique exercises guide students in assessing their understanding of the sources, in organizing those sources for use in an essay, and in drawing useful conclusions from them. In this interactive learning environment, students will enhance their ability to build arguments and to practice historical reasoning.

More specifically, a short **quiz after each source** offers students the opportunity to check their understanding of materials that often derive from quite distant times and places. Some questions focus on audience, purpose, point of view, limitations, or context, while others challenge students to draw conclusions about the source or to compare one source with another. Immediate substantive feedback for each rejoinder and the opportunity to try again create an active learning environment where students are rewarded for reaching the correct answer through their own process of exploration.

Two activities at the end of each Thinking through Sources exercise ask students to make supportable inferences and draw appropriate conclusions from sources with reference to a **Guiding Question**. In the **Organize the Evidence activity**, students identify which sources provide evidence for a topic that would potentially compose part of an answer to the guiding question. In the **Draw Conclusions from the Evidence activity**, students assess whether a specific piece of evidence drawn from the sources supports or challenges a conclusion related to the guiding question. Collectively these assignments create an active learning environment where reading with a purpose is reinforced by immediate feedback and support. The guiding question provides a foundation for in-class activities or a summative writing assignment.

To learn more about the benefits of LaunchPad and the different versions of *Ways of the World* to package with LaunchPad, visit **macmillanhighered.com /strayersources/catalog**.

Acknowledgments

We extend our thanks to acquiring editor Laura Arcari, senior development editor Leah Strauss, senior production editor Christina Horn, and assistant production editor Erica Zhang of Bedford/St. Martin's.

Robert Strayer, La Selva Beach, California, Winter 2016
Eric Nelson, Springfield, Missouri, Winter 2016

Contents

17 Experiencing the Early Industrial Revolution   73

18 Colonial India: Experience and Response   86

19 Japan and the West in the Nineteenth Century   100

20 Experiencing World War I   114

21 Experiencing Stalinism   126

CHAPTER 12

Early Encounters; First Impressions

During the fifteenth century on the remote far western end of the Eurasian landmass, the government of Portugal initiated a series of maritime explorations with profound implications for the entire world. Spain and other European powers soon followed suit. Their voyages down the coast of West Africa, around the Cape of Good Hope to India, and across the Atlantic to the Americas set in motion a pattern of European expansion that by 1900 had enveloped most of the peoples of the planet — with incalculable consequences that continue to echo to this day. In that epic process, the peoples of Europe and those of Africa, Asia, and the Americas encountered one another in new ways and often for the first time. Here we examine three of these early encounters and the impressions they generated. The limitations of available sources unfortunately dictate a largely Eurocentric focus, for we know much more about how Europeans experienced these encounters than we do about how the people they met experienced them. Everyone, however, shared an inability to imagine the enormously transforming, and often devastating, outcomes of these early interactions. But here our attention is focused on the initial moments of these historic encounters, pregnant as they were with implications for the future.

Source 12.1
Cadamosto in a West African Chiefdom

At the beginning of the fifteenth century, no one could have predicted that the small and poor kingdom of Portugal, operating at the margins of European life, would become a major international power over the next two centuries. But building on a long seafaring tradition in Mediterranean and North African waters, the Portuguese royal family sponsored a series of maritime voyages that took them down the coast of West Africa and in 1498 all the way to India. A global Portuguese empire began to take shape. It was driven by a familiar mixture of motives — to seek a sea route to the luxury goods of the East; to outflank, defeat, and if possible convert Muslims; to ally with any Christians they could find to continue the crusades; and to provide aristocratic warriors an opportunity for military glory and social promotion. These voyages produced any number of first encounters between Europeans and various African societies as the Portuguese explored the region, constructed trading posts and forts, sought gold and slaves, and made modest efforts at missionary activity.

Among the earliest and the most carefully recorded of these first encounters occurred in 1455, when the Italian trader and explorer Alvise da Cadamosto, sailing for Portugal, encountered Budomel, the ruler of a small chiefdom within the Wolof-speaking state of Cayor in what is now Senegal. The two men apparently hit it off, for Budomel soon invited Cadamosto to visit his residence about 25 miles inland. Observant and open-minded, Cadamosto later wrote an account of his month-long visit, which has become an important source for historians of fifteenth-century West Africa. In doing so, he also recorded one of the earliest encounters between European explorers and black Africans.

Questions to consider as you examine the source:

- How would you describe Cadamosto's posture toward Budomel and his society? What did he admire? What did he criticize? In what ways was he judging it by European standards?

- How might Budomel have written about his encounter with Cadamosto?

- What could historians learn from this account about this West African society in the mid-fifteenth century? Consider the role of slavery, the position of women, the political system, economic transactions, the penetration of Islam, and relationships with a wider world.

ALVISE DA CADAMOSTO
On Meeting with Budomel
1455

This is what I was able to observe. . . . First, I saw clearly that, though these pass as lords, it must not be thought that they have castles or cities. . . . The King of this realm had nothing save villages of grass huts, and Budomel was lord only of a part of this realm. . . . Such men are not lords by virtue of treasure or money, for they possess neither, but on account of ceremonies and the following of people they may truly be called lords; indeed they receive beyond comparison more obedience than our lords.

The dwelling of such a King is never fixed: he has a number of villages to support his wives and families. In the village where I was, . . . there were from forty to fifty grass huts close together in a circle, surrounded by hedges and groves of great trees, leaving but one or two gaps as entrances. Each hut has a yard divided off by hedges. . . . In this place Budomel had nine wives: and likewise in his other dwellings, according to his will and pleasure. Each of these wives has five or six young negro girls in attendance upon her, and it is as lawful for the lord to sleep with these attendants as with his wives, to whom this does not appear an injury, for it is customary.

These negroes, both men and women, are exceedingly lascivious: Budomel demanded of me importunately, having been given to understand that Christians knew how to do many things, whether by chance I could give him the means by which he could satisfy many women, for which he offered me a great reward.

This Budomel always has at least two hundred negroes with him, who constantly follow him.... [T]he nearer one approaches the apartment of Budomel, the greater is the dignity of those living in these courts, up to the door of Budomel.

This Budomel exhibits haughtiness, showing himself only for an hour in the morning, and for a short while towards evening.... Such lords as he, when granting audience to anyone, display much ceremony: however considerable he who seeks audience may be, or however high born, on entering the door of Budomel's courtyard he throws himself down on his knees, bows his head to the ground, and with both hands scatters sand upon his naked shoulders and head.... No man would be bold enough to come before him to parley, unless he had stripped himself naked save for the girdle of leather they wear.

All this appears to me to proceed from the great fear and dread in which these people hold their lord, since for the most trivial misdeed he seizes and sells their wives and children. Thus it appears to me that his power exacts obedience and fear from the people by selling their wives and children. In two ways they exercise the rights of lords, and display power, that is, in maintaining a train of followers, in allowing themselves to be seen rarely, and in being greatly reverenced by their subjects....

I was permitted to enter the mosque where they pray: arriving towards evening, and having called those of his ... Arabs (those who are learned in the laws of Muhammad), he entered with some of his chief lords into a certain place. There they prayed in this fashion: standing upright and frequently looking up to the sky, they took two paces forward, and recited some words in a low voice: then bowed down very often and kissed the earth.... And thus they continued for the space of half an hour. [*Note: Cadamosto witnessed the* salat, *the ritual prayer of Islam.*]

When he had finished, he asked me what I thought of it.... Finally I told him that his faith was false, and that those who had instructed him in such things were ignorant of the truth. On many grounds I proved his faith to be false and our faith to be true and holy, thus getting the better of his learned men in argument.... The lord laughed at this, saying that our faith appeared to him to be good: for it could be no other than God that had bestowed so many good and rich gifts and so much skill and knowledge upon us.... He was much pleased with the actions of the Christians, and I am certain it would have been easy to have converted him to the Christian faith, if he had not feared to lose his power.

Each of his wives sends him a certain number of dishes of food every day. All the negro lords and men of this land follow this fashion, their women supplying them with food. They eat on the ground, like animals, without manners. No one eats with these negro rulers, save those Moors [North African Muslims] who teach the law, and one or two of their chief men.

[After learning about a snake-charming ritual], I conclude that all these negroes are great magicians; and others could bear witness to the truth of this charming of the snakes....

I decided to go to see a market.... This was held in a field, on Mondays and Fridays. Men and women came to it from the neighbourhood country within a distance of four or five miles, for those who dwelt farther off attended other markets. In this market I perceived quite clearly that these people are exceedingly poor, judging from the wares they brought for sale: that is, cotton, but not in large quantities, cotton thread and cloth, vegetables, oil and millet, wooden bowls, palm leaf mats, and all the other articles they use in their daily life. Men as well as women came to sell, some of the men offering their weapons, and others a little gold, but not in any quantity. They sold everything, item by item, by barter, and not for money, for they have none. They do not use money of any kind, but barter only, one thing for another, two for one, three for two.

These negroes, men and women, crowded to see me as though I were a marvel. It seemed to be a new experience to them to see Christians, whom they had not previously seen. They marvelled no less at my clothing than at my white skin. . . . Some touched my hands and limbs, and rubbed me with their spittle to discover whether my whiteness was dye or flesh. Finding that it was flesh they were astounded.

Horses are highly prized in this country of the Blacks, because they are to be had only with great difficulty, for they are brought from our Barbary [North Africa] by the Arabs and . . . cannot withstand the great heat. A horse with its trappings is sold for from nine to fourteen negro slaves, according to the condition and breeding of the horse. When a chief buys a horse, he sends for his horse-charmers, who have a great fire of certain herbs lighted after their fashion, which makes a great smoke. Into this they lead the horse by the bridle, muttering their spells. . . . Then they fasten to its neck charms [probably containing passages from the Quran]. . . . They believe that with these they are safer in battle.

The women of this country are very pleasant and light-hearted, ready to sing and to dance, especially the young girls. They dance, however, only at night by the light of the moon. Their dances are very different from ours.

These negroes marvelled greatly at many of our possessions, particularly at our crossbows, and, above all, our mortars. Some came to the ship, and I had them shown the firing of a mortar, the noise of which frightened them exceedingly. I then told them that a mortar would slay more than a hundred men at one shot, at which they were astonished, saying that it was an invention of the devil's. . . .

When I had despatched my business, and had acquired a certain number of slaves, I decided to continue beyond Capo Verde, to discover new lands, and to make good my venture.

Source: G. R. Crone, *The Voyages of Cadamosto and Other Documents on Western Africa* (Farnham, Surrey, GBR: Hakluyt Society, 1937), 35–52. Used by permission of the Hakluyt Society.

Source 12.2
Vasco da Gama at Calicut, India

On May 20, 1498, the Portuguese marked a major milestone in over eighty years of voyaging down the west coast of Africa when Vasco da Gama led a small fleet of four ships around the Cape of Good Hope, across the Indian Ocean, arriving at the south Indian port city of Calicut. That event represented the first direct entry of Europeans into the long-established network of Indian Ocean commerce from which they had long obtained precious spices, gemstones, and other luxury goods, albeit only through Muslim intermediaries. Now they were directly operating within this complex, international system of exchange, much of it dominated by Muslims. Commercial desires combined with an anti-Muslim crusading sensibility to fuel Portuguese entry into what was for them another "New World."

When da Gama arrived, the coast of southwestern India hosted a number of small states, cities, and kingdoms, fierce rivals for the rich profits of trade in spices and especially pepper. Calicut, the most prominent of these states, was ruled by Hindus, but Arab Muslims were the most strongly established trading community operating in the city. Both economic interest and religious hostility to Christians ensured that they did not look favorably on the arrival of da Gama.

This initial encounter lasted about three months, much of it recorded in an official journal of da Gama's voyage compiled by an unknown author. Excerpts from the journal provide a flavor of that encounter, obviously from a Portuguese perspective, but "between the lines" we can perhaps discern other perspectives as well.

Questions to consider as you examine the source:

■ How might you summarize the motivations and hopes that animated da Gama's voyage? To what extent were they fulfilled?

■ How did da Gama explain the difficulties he faced in Calicut? Can you think of other possible explanations for these problems?

■ The ruler of Calicut at times seems quite welcoming to da Gama and at other times suspicious and hostile. How might you explain this ambivalence?

A Journal of the First Voyage of Vasco da Gama
1498

[*The first sustained interaction between da Gama and local people occurred in an encounter with two Arab Muslims from Tunis, who could speak Spanish and Italian.*]

The first greeting that he [da Gama] received was in these words: "May the Devil take thee! What brought you hither?" They asked what he sought so far away from home, and he told them that we came in search of Christians and of spices. . . . [One of the Muslims] said these words: "A lucky venture. . . . Plenty of rubies, plenty of emeralds! You owe great thanks to God, for having brought you to a country holding such riches!" We were greatly astonished to hear his talk, for we never expected to hear our language spoken so far away from Portugal. . . .

[*A few days later, da Gama traveled inland for an audience with the ruler of Calicut. The journal notes that* his party observed "many large ships," huge crowds of curious people, and an elaborate "church," most likely a Hindu temple. The Portuguese initially mistook Hindus for Christians, perhaps because they had heard rumors of a small Christian community, allegedly derived from the early missionary work of Saint Thomas, that did in fact live in southern India.]

On landing, the captain-major [da Gama] was received by [an official], with whom were many men, armed and unarmed. The reception was friendly, as if the people were pleased to see us, though at first appearances looked threatening, for they carried naked swords in their hands. A palanquin [a covered chair carried on poles by four men] was provided for the captain-major, such as is used by men of distinction in that country. . . .

The king was in a small court, reclining upon a couch covered with a cloth of green velvet, above which was a good mattress, and upon this again a sheet of cotton stuff, very white and fine. . . . The king . . . asked the captain-major what he wanted. And the captain-major told him he was the ambassador of a King of Portugal, who was Lord of many countries and the possessor of great wealth of every description, exceeding that of any king of these parts; that for a period of sixty years his ancestors had annually sent out vessels to make discoveries in the direction of India, as they knew that there were Christian kings there like themselves. This, he said, was the reason which induced them to order this country to be discovered, not because they sought for gold or silver, for of this they had such abundance that they needed not what was to be found in this country.

[*This visit seemed to go well, but the next day, when da Gama was preparing gifts for the king, several officials came to inspect the gifts.*]

They came, and when they saw the present they laughed at it, saying that it was not a thing to offer to a king, that the poorest merchant from Mecca, or any other part of India, gave more, and that if he wanted to make a present it should be in gold, as the king would not accept such things. . . .

[*The next day, the king kept da Gama waiting for four hours and then belittled Portuguese goods.*]

The king then said that he [da Gama] had told him that he came from a very rich kingdom, and yet had brought him nothing. . . . The king then asked what it was he had come to discover: stones [gems] or men? If he came to discover men, as he said, why had he brought nothing? The king then asked what kind of merchandise was to be found in his country. The captain-major said there was much corn, cloth, iron, bronze, and many other things. The king asked whether he had any merchandise with him. The captain-major replied that he had a little of each sort, as samples, and that if permitted to return to the ships he would order it to be landed. . . . The king said no! He might take all his people with him, securely moor his ships, land his merchandise, and sell it to the best advantage [in the private market]. . . . [But even in this private trading], we did not, however, effect these

sales at the prices hoped for when we arrived . . . , for a very fine shirt which in Portugal fetches 300 reis, was worth here only 30 reis. And just as we sold shirts cheaply so we sold other things, in order to take some things away from this country, if only for samples. Those who visited the city bought there cloves, cinnamon, and precious stones.

[*The Portuguese had little doubt as to the source of this apparent hostility.*]

We also felt grieved that a Christian [actually a Hindu] king, to whom we had given of ours, should do us such an ill turn. At the same time we did not hold him as culpable as he seemed to be, for we were well aware that the Moors [Muslims] of the place, who were merchants from Mecca and elsewhere, could ill digest us. They had told the king that we were thieves, and that if once we navigated to his country, no more ships from Mecca, nor . . . any other part, would visit him. They added that he would derive no profit from this [trade with Portugal] as we had nothing to give, but would rather take away, and that thus his country would be ruined. They, moreover, offered rich bribes to the king to capture and kill us, so that we should not return to Portugal.

[*What followed was a series of controversies about the unloading of da Gama's ships, the mutual seizure of hostages, the payment required before leaving Calicut, and more. Several minor naval engagements showed da Gama that even if his goods were not so appealing, his on-board artillery far surpassed anything available locally. When he arrived home, da Gama found a very pleased king of Portugal, who wrote with pleasure to the monarchs of Spain about da Gama's achievement.*]

[W]e learn that they did reach and discover India and other kingdoms and lordships bordering upon it; that they entered and navigated its sea, finding large cities, large edifices and rivers, and great populations, among whom is carried on all the trade in spices and precious stones, which are forwarded in ships . . . to Mecca, and thence to Cairo, whence they are dispersed throughout the world. Of these [spices, etc.] they have brought a quantity, including cinnamon, cloves, ginger, nutmeg, and pepper as well as other kinds, together with the boughs and leaves of the same; also many fine stones of all sorts, such as rubies and others.

And they also came to a country in which there are mines of gold. . . .

[W]hat we have learnt concerning the Christian people whom these explorers reached [is] that it will be possible, notwithstanding that they are not as yet strong in the faith or possessed of a thorough knowledge of it, to do much in the service of God and the exaltation of the Holy Faith, once they shall have been converted and fully fortified (confirmed) in it. And when they shall have thus been fortified in the faith there will be an opportunity for destroying the Moors of those parts. Moreover we hope, with the help of God that the great trade which now enriches the Moors of those parts . . . , shall, in consequence of our regulations, be diverted to the natives and ships of our own kingdom.

Source: E. G. Ravenstein, trans., *A Journal of the First Voyage of Vasco da Gama, 1497–1499* (London: Hakluyt Society, 1898), https://openlibrary.org/books/OL6912713M/A_journal_of_the _first_voyage_of_Vasco_da_Gama_1497-1499.

Source 12.3
Celebrating da Gama's Arrival in Calicut

The extraordinary feats of navigation accomplished by Portuguese sailors gave their kingdom a new prominence on the European stage. Portuguese rulers publicized their accomplishments by displaying the exotic products from the East to a European public hungry for information about distant lands. Perhaps no single item brought back from India created a greater stir than the live rhinoceros that arrived in 1515. Crowds flocked in amazement to view a beast that had not been seen in Europe for over 1,000 years and was only known through an account by the ancient Roman scholar Pliny.

The most systematic effort to associate the Portuguese monarchy with the opening of the East took the form of a twenty-six-panel series of tapestries commemorating da Gama's 1498 voyage to Calicut. Commissioned by King Manuel in 1504, these expensive woven works of art were intended to hang in the great hall of the royal palace where official business was conducted. The scenes incorporate a wide variety of exotica, including dark-skinned people dressed in elaborate, if often inaccurate, costumes and rare or mythical animals. Woven in the Low Countries (modern day Belgium and the Netherlands), by artisans who had never seen their subjects, the tapestries feature many scenes containing fanciful elements, while other scenes draw on more familiar topics, including classical accounts of Alexander the Great's conquests in the East. Nevertheless, these tapestries proved influential in shaping European conceptions of India, as the same artisans produced many copies and variations on these panels for other European elites fascinated by the Portuguese discoveries.

The panel reproduced here depicts the arrival of da Gama at Calicut. The scene includes accurate renderings of Portuguese vessels anchored in the port; however, the buildings and town gates of Calicut are more fanciful, constructed out of distinctly European, not Indian, architectural elements. In the foreground to the left, da Gama presents a letter from his monarch to the ruler of Calicut. In the center of the scene, the Portuguese are in the process of unloading from their vessels exotic animals, including ostriches, wild cats, and even a unicorn. To the right, a great crowd dressed in garments reminiscent of European styles gathers to view these curiosities, very much like the Europeans who gathered to view the Indian rhinoceros unloaded in Lisbon harbor in 1515.

Questions to consider as you examine the source:

- In what ways does this image reflect the written account in Source 12.2? In what ways does it differ?

- How does this tapestry serve the purposes of King Manuel of Portugal, who commissioned it?

- What can you discern about European knowledge of India from this image?

The Arrival of da Gama at Calicut

Museu Nacional de Arte Antiga, Lisbon, Portugal/Alfred Dagli Orti/Art Resource, NY

Source 12.4
Columbus in the Caribbean

Even apart from its horrific long-term consequences, Columbus's arrival in the Caribbean region in October of 1492 retains a distinctive significance. Europeans were at least aware of Asian and African societies and had experienced some interaction, often indirect, with them. But except for the brief and unremembered incursions of the Vikings, no one from the Afro-Eurasian hemisphere had set foot in the Americas since the last migrants from Siberia had crossed the Bering Strait perhaps 15,000 years earlier. So the arrival of Columbus was an extraordinary encounter.

Columbus's voyage, sponsored by the monarchs of Spain, found a densely settled agricultural people known as the Taino inhabiting the islands now called Hispaniola (modern Haiti and Dominican Republic), Cuba, Jamaica, and Puerto Rico. Organized into substantial village communities governed by a hierarchy of chiefs (*cacique*), Taino society featured modest class distinctions. An elite group of chiefs, warriors, artists, and religious specialists enjoyed a higher status than did commoners, who worked the fields, fished, and hunted.

On the voyage back to Europe in early 1493, Columbus penned a letter to Lord Raphael Sanchez, a prominent official in the government of his patrons, King Ferdinand and Queen Isabella of Spain. In it he summarized his initial impressions and his hopes for the future for both Sanchez and his royal patrons.

Questions to consider as you examine the source:

■ What can you infer from the letter about Columbus's expectations for his journey and what he wanted from his Spanish patrons?

■ Scholars have noted a number of omissions from Columbus's letter: that one of his ships had been lost; that some of his men had abused local women; that he had had at least one violent encounter with local people; that his ability to communicate with the Taino was minimal. Why might he have omitted these incidents?

■ How might you summarize Columbus's posture toward the people he met on this first voyage? Can you see ways in which he was trying to "spin" his description of these people? Did he have preconceptions that may have colored his understanding of them?

CHRISTOPHER COLUMBUS

Letter to Ferdinand and Isabella

1493

Thirty-three days after my departure from Cadiz [in Spain] I reached the Indian [Caribbean] sea, where I discovered many islands, thickly peopled, of which I took possession without resistance in the name of our most illustrious Monarch, by public proclamation and with unfurled banners . . . ; to each of these I also gave a name, ordering that one should be called Santa Maria de la Concepcion, another Fernandina, the third Isabella, the fourth Juana, and so with all the rest respectively.

As soon as we arrived at Juana, I proceeded along its coast a short distance. . . . I could not suppose it to be an island, but the continental province of Cathay [China]. Seeing, however, no towns or populous places on the sea coast, but only a few detached houses and cottages, with whose inhabitants I was unable to communicate, because they fled as soon as they saw us, I went further on, thinking that in my progress I should certainly find some city or village. . . . I afterwards dispatched two of our men to ascertain whether there were a king or any cities in that province. These men reconnoitered the country for three days, and found a most numerous population, and great numbers of houses, though small, and built without any regard to order. . . .

The inhabitants of both sexes in this island, and in all the others which I have seen, go always naked as they were born, with the exception of some of the women, who use the covering of a leaf, or small bough, or an apron of cotton. . . . None of them . . . are possessed of any iron, neither have they weapons, being unacquainted with, and indeed incompetent to use them, not from any deformity of body (for they are well-formed), but because they are timid and full of fear. . . . This timidity did not arise from any loss or injury that they had received from us; for, on the contrary, I gave to all I approached whatever articles I had about me, such as cloth and many other things,

taking nothing of theirs in return. . . . As soon however as they see that they are safe, and have laid aside all fear, they are very simple and honest, and exceedingly liberal with all they have; none of them refusing anything he may possess when he is asked for it, but on the contrary inviting us to ask them. They exhibit great love towards all others in preference to themselves: they also give objects of great value for trifles. . . .

Thus they bartered, like idiots, cotton and gold for fragments of bows, glasses, bottles, and jars; which I forbad as being unjust, and myself gave them many beautiful and acceptable articles which I had brought with me, taking nothing from them in return; I did this in order that I might the more easily conciliate them, that they might be led to become Christians, and be inclined to entertain a regard for the King and Queen, our Princes and all Spaniards, and that I might induce them to take an interest in seeking out, and collecting, and delivering to us such things as they possessed in abundance, but which we greatly needed.

They practice no kind of idolatry, but have a firm belief that all strength and power, and indeed all good things, are in heaven, and that I had descended from thence with these ships and sailors, and under this impression was I received after they had thrown aside their fears. Nor are they slow or stupid, but of very clear understanding; and those men who have crossed to the neighbouring islands give an admirable description of everything they observed; but they never saw any people clothed, nor any ships like ours.

On my arrival at that sea, I had taken some Indians by force from the first island that I came to, in order that they might learn our language, and communicate to us what they knew respecting the country; which plan succeeded excellently, and was a great advantage to us, for in a short time, either by gestures and signs, or by words, we were enabled to understand each other.

Each of these islands has a great number of canoes, built of solid wood, narrow. . . . These canoes are of various sizes, but the greater number are constructed with eighteen banks of oars, and with these they cross to the other islands. . . . I took possession of all these islands in the name of our invincible King, yet there was one large town in Espanola of which especially I took possession, situated . . . in every way convenient for the purposes of gain and commerce.

To this town I gave the name of Navidad del Senor, and ordered a fortress to be built there, I also . . . engaged the favor and friendship of the King of the island . . . , for these people are so amiable and friendly that even the King took a pride in calling me his brother. . . . [T]hose who hold the said fortress, can easily keep the whole island in check, without any pressing danger to themselves. . . .

As far as I have learned, every man throughout these islands is united to but one wife, with the exception of the kings and princes, who are allowed to have twenty: the women seem to work more than the men. I could not clearly understand whether the people possess any private property, for I observed that one man had the charge of distributing various things to the rest, but especially meat and provisions and the like. . . .

[I]n a certain island called Charis . . . dwell a people who are considered by the neighbouring islanders as most ferocious: and these feed upon human flesh. The same people have many kinds of canoes, in which they cross to all the surrounding islands and rob and plunder wherever they can. . . . These are the men who form unions with certain women, who dwell alone in the island Matenin, which lies next to Espanola on the side towards India; these latter [women] employ themselves in no labour suitable to their own sex, for they use bows and javelins as I have already described their paramours as doing. . . .

I promise, that with a little assistance afforded me by our most invincible sovereigns, I will procure them as much gold as they need, as great a quantity of spices, of cotton, and of mastic . . . , and as many men [slaves] for the service of the navy as their Majesties may require. I promise also rhubarb and other sorts of drugs. . . . Although all I have related may appear to be wonderful and unheard of, yet the results of my voyage would have been more astonishing if I had had at my disposal such ships as I required. But these great and marvellous results are not to be attributed to any merit of mine, but to the holy Christian faith, and to the piety and religion of our Sovereigns. . . . Thus it has happened to me in the present instance, who have accomplished a task to which the powers of mortal men had never hitherto attained.

Source: Christopher Columbus, letter to Lord Raphael Sanchez (treasurer to Ferdinand and Isabella), 14 March 1493, The Internet Modern History Sourcebook, Fordham University, accessed June 1, 2015, http://www2.fiu.edu/~harveyb/colum.html.

Source 12.5
Columbus Engraved

Precisely a century after Columbus first arrived in the Americas, the Flemish artist Theodore de Bry depicted his landing in an engraving that has become an iconic image of that event. While some elements of the engraving are accurate, including the ships, the raising of a cross, and the dress of Columbus's men, others are fanciful, like the jewelry, ornate vessels, and chests, all made of gold and in European Renaissance styles, that the Taino offer Columbus.

Questions to consider as you examine the source:

■ How does de Bry portray Columbus's assertion of authority in a land so far from his own?

■ How does the artist differentiate between the Europeans and the Taino?

■ How would you summarize the "message" of this image?

Columbus Arriving on Hispaniola

From *Americae Tertia Pars IV*, 1594/bpk, Berlin/Art Resource, NY

ESSAY QUESTIONS

Early Encounters; First Impressions

1. **Comparing first encounters:** How would you compare the first impressions that these three encounters generated for the Europeans involved? What surprised them? What offended their sensibilities? How did they describe or portray cultural differences? How open to these differences did they seem to be?

2. **Establishing political ties:** What political relationship with the host society did each of the Europeans have? What were they seeking from those societies? To what extent did these factors shape their posture toward those they were meeting for the first time?

3. **Reading between the lines:** Although these sources all derive from Europeans, what might we infer, reading between the lines, about how the West African, Indian, and Native American figures may have understood these encounters?

4. **Foreshadowing future encounters:** In what ways did these encounters bear the seeds of future developments, although unknown to everyone at the time?

CHAPTER 13

THINKING THROUGH SOURCES

The Spanish and the Aztecs: From Encounter to Conquest (1519–1521)

Among the sagas of early modern empire building, few have been more dramatic, more tragic, or better documented than the Spanish conquest of the Aztec Empire during the early sixteenth century. In recounting this story, historians are fortunate in having considerable evidence from both the Spanish and the Aztec sides of the encounter.

Source 13.1
The Meeting of Cortés and Moctezuma: A Spanish View

In February 1519, twenty-seven years after Columbus first claimed a New World for Spain, Hernán Cortés, accompanied by some 350 Spanish soldiers, set off from Cuba with a fleet of eleven ships, stopping at several places along the Gulf of Mexico before proceeding to march inland toward Tenochtitlán (teh-noch-TEE-lan), the capital of the Aztec Empire. Along the way, he learned something about the fabulous wealth of this empire and about the fragility of its political structure. He also received various emissaries from the Aztec ruler Moctezuma, bearing rich gifts and warm greetings. Through a combination of force and astute diplomacy, Cortés was able to negotiate alliances with a number of the Aztecs' restive subject peoples and with the Aztecs' many rivals or enemies, especially the Tlaxcalans. With his modest forces thus greatly reinforced, Cortés arrived on November 8, 1519, in Tenochtitlán, where his famous meeting with Moctezuma took place. Bernal Díaz, a Spanish soldier who took part in the expedition, recounted his recollection of this encounter some thirty years later.

Questions to consider as you examine the source:

■ How would you describe the Spanish posture toward the Aztecs? What amazed them and what appalled them?

■ Does the account by Díaz confirm or challenge the controversial notion that the Aztecs viewed the Spanish as divine beings of some kind?

■ What differences in religious understanding emerged in the conversations between the two leaders? Were there any areas of agreement?

BERNAL DÍAZ
The True History of the Conquest of New Spain
Mid-Sixteenth Century

We proceeded along the Causeway which . . . runs straight to the City of Mexico. It was so crowded with people that there was hardly room for them all. They had never before seen horses or men such as we are.

Gazing on such wonderful sights, we did not know what to say, . . . for on one side, on the land, there were great cities, and in the lake ever so many more, and the lake itself was crowded with canoes, and in the Causeway were many bridges at intervals, and in front of us stood the great City of Mexico, and we, — we did not even number four hundred soldiers!

When we arrived, . . . many more chieftains and Caciques approached clad in very rich mantles. The Great Moctezuma had sent these great Caciques in advance to receive us, and when they came before Cortés they bade us welcome in their language, and as a sign of peace, they touched their hands against the ground, and kissed the ground with the hand.

When we arrived near to Mexico, the Great Moctezuma got down from his litter, and those great Caciques supported him with their arms beneath a marvellously rich canopy of green coloured feathers with much gold and silver embroidery and with pearls suspended from a sort of bordering, which was wonderful to look at. Besides these four Chieftains, there were four other great Caciques, who supported the canopy over their heads, and many other Lords who walked before the Great Moctezuma, sweeping the ground where he would tread and spreading cloths on it, so that he should not tread on the earth. Not one of these chieftains dared even to think of looking him in the face, but kept their eyes lowered with great reverence, except those four relations, his nephews, who supported him with their arms.

When Cortés was told that the Great Moctezuma was approaching, he dismounted from his horse, and when he was near Moctezuma, they simultaneously paid great reverence to one another. Moctezuma bade him welcome, and our Cortés replied through Doña Marina wishing him very good health. And it seems to me that Cortés, through Doña Marina, offered him his right hand, and Moctezuma did not wish to take it, but he did give his hand to Cortés and Cortés brought out a necklace which he had ready at hand, made of glass stones, . . . and he placed it round the neck of the Great Moctezuma and when he had so placed it he was going to embrace him, and those great Princes who accompanied Moctezuma held back Cortés by the arm so that he should not embrace him, for they considered it an indignity.

Then Cortés through the mouth of Doña Marina told him that now his heart rejoiced at having seen such a great Prince, and that he took it as a great honour that he had come in person to meet him and had frequently shown him such favour. Then Moctezuma spoke other words of politeness to him, and told two of his nephews . . . to go with us and show us to our quarters. . . . They took us to lodge in some large houses, where there were apartments for all of us. . . . They took us to lodge in that house, because they called us Teules [the Spanish took this word to mean "gods"], and took us for such, so that we should be with the Idols or Teules which were kept there. . . .

[*After a "sumptuous dinner" and more "polite speech," everyone retired for the night. The next day Cortés and Moctezuma met again and exchanged views on religion. After Cortés outlined the basics of the Christian faith, he invited Moctezuma to embrace it.*]

[Cortés told] how such a brother as our great Emperor, grieving for the perdition of so many souls, such as those which their idols were leading to Hell, where they burn in living flames, had sent us, so that after what he [Moctezuma] had now heard he would put a stop to it and they would no longer adore these Idols or sacrifice Indian men and women to them, for we were all brethren, nor should they commit sodomy or thefts. . . . At present we merely came to give them due warning, and so he prayed him to do what he was asked and carry it into effect.

Moctezuma replied — "Señor Malinche, I have understood your words and arguments very well before now, from what you said to my servants. . . . We have not made any answer to it because here throughout all time we have worshipped our own gods, and thought they were good, as no doubt yours are, so do not trouble to speak to us any more about them at present. Regarding the creation of the world, we have held the same belief for ages past, and for this reason we take it for certain that you are those whom our ancestors predicted would come from the direction of the sunrise. As for your great King, I feel that I am indebted to him, and I will give him of what I possess. . . .

And Moctezuma said, laughing, for he was very merry in his princely way of speaking: "Malinche, I know very well that these people of Tlaxcala with whom you are such good friends have told you that I am a sort of God or Teul, and that everything in my houses is made of gold and silver and precious stones, I know well enough that you are wise and did not believe it but took it as a joke. Behold now, Señor Malinche, my body is of flesh and bone like yours, my houses and palaces of stone and wood and lime; that I am a great king and inherit the riches of my ancestors is true, but not all the nonsense and lies that they have told you about me, although of course you treated it as a joke, as I did your thunder and lightning."

[*A few days later Cortés asked Moctezuma to "show us your gods and Teules." On a visit to the main temple, Díaz described the many grotesquely carved "idols" and recalled evidence of recent human sacrifices.*]

They had offered to this Idol five hearts from that day's sacrifices. . . . Everything was covered with blood, both walls and altar, and the stench was such that we could hardly wait the moment to get out of it.

Our Captain said to Moctezuma through our interpreter, half laughing: "Señor Moctezuma, I do not understand how such a great Prince and wise man as you are has not come to the conclusion, in your mind, that these idols of yours are not gods, but evil things that are called devils, and so that you may know it and all your priests may see it clearly, do me the favour to approve of my placing a cross . . . [and] divide off a space where we can set up an image of Our Lady."

Moctezuma replied half angrily (and the two priests who were with him showed great annoyance), and said: "Señor Malinche, if I had known that you would have said such defamatory things I would not have shown you my gods, we consider them to be very good, for they give us health and rains and good seed times and seasons and as many victories as we desire, and we are obliged to worship them and make sacrifices, and I pray you not to say another word to their dishonour."

When our Captain heard that and noted the angry looks he did not refer again to the subject, but said with a cheerful manner: "It is time for your Excellency and for us to return." And Moctezuma replied that it was well, but that he had to pray and offer certain sacrifices on account of the great tatacul, that is to say sin, which he had committed in allowing us to ascend his great Cue [temple], and being the cause of our being permitted to see his gods, and of our dishonouring them by speaking evil of them, so that before he left he must pray and worship.

Then Cortés said "I ask your pardon if it be so. . . ." After our Captain and all of us were tired of walking about and seeing such a diversity of Idols and their sacrifices, we returned to our quarters.

Source: Bernal Díaz, *The True History of the Conquest of New Spain* (London Hakluyt Society, 1908). Excerpt taken from Bedford series book Stuart B. Schwartz, *Victors and Vanquished* (Boston: Bedford/St. Martin's, 2000), pp. 133–55.

Source 13.2
The Meeting of Cortés and Moctezuma: An Aztec Account

Another account of this initial encounter comes from *The Florentine Codex*, a compilation of text and images, compiled under the leadership of Fray Bernardino de Sahagún, a Franciscan missionary who believed that an understanding of Aztec culture was essential to the task of conversion. Because Sahagún relied on Aztec informants and artists, many scholars believe that *The Florentine Codex* and other codices represent indigenous understandings of the conquest. However, they require a critical reading. They date from several decades after the events they describe. Many contributors to the codices had been influenced by the Christian and European culture of their missionary mentors, and they were writing or painting in a society thoroughly dominated by Spanish colonial rule. Furthermore, the codices reflect the ethnic and regional diversity of Mesoamerica rather than a single Aztec perspective. Despite such limitations, these codices represent a unique window into Mesoamerican understandings of the conquest.

Questions to consider as you examine the source:

- How does this account differ from that of Díaz (Source 13.1)? In what ways does it overlap or supplement Díaz's understanding?

- What in particular did the author of this report notice about the Spanish?

- This text and that of Díaz were composed some thirty years or so after the events they describe. How might this fact affect our understanding of these documents?

FRAY BERNARDINO DE SAHAGÚN
The Florentine Codex
Mid-Sixteenth Century

Then they [the Spaniards] set out in this direction, about to enter Mexico [the city of Tenochtitlán] here. Then they all dressed and equipped themselves for war. They girded themselves, tying their battle gear lightly on themselves and then on their horses. Then they arranged themselves in rows, files, ranks. . . . They kept turning about as they went, facing people, looking this way and that, looking sideways, gazing everywhere between the houses, examining things, looking up at the roofs.

By himself came marching ahead, all alone, the one who bore the standard [flag] on his shoulder. . . . Following him came those with iron swords. Their iron swords came bare and gleaming.

The second contingent and file were horses carrying people, each with his cotton cuirass [armor], his leather shield, his iron lance, and his iron sword hanging down from the horse's neck. They came with bells on, jingling or rattling. The deer [horses] neighed, there was much neighing. . . . Their hooves made holes, they dug holes in the ground wherever they placed them. . . .

The third file were those with iron crossbows. As they came, the iron crossbows lay in their arms. They came along testing them out, brandishing them, (aiming them). . . .

The fourth file were likewise [horsemen].

The fifth group were those with harquebuses [crude guns]. . . . And when they went into the great palace, the residence of the ruler, they repeatedly shot off their harquebuses. They exploded, sputtered, discharged, thundered. Smoke spread. . . . The fetid smell made people dizzy and faint.

And last, bringing up the rear, went the war leader, thought to be the ruler and director in battle. . . . Gathered and massed about him, going at his side, accompanying him, enclosing him were his warriors, the strong and valiant ones of the altepetl [a region or city].

Then all those from the various altepetl on the other side of the mountains, the Tlaxcalans, the people of Tliliuhquitepec, of Huexotzinco, came following behind. They came outfitted for war. . . . Some bore burdens and provisions on their backs. . . . Some dragged the large cannons, which went resting on wooden wheels, making a clamor as they came.

And when they [the Spaniards] had come as far as Xoloco, when they had stopped there, Moctezuma dressed and prepared himself for a meeting, along with other great rulers and high nobles, his rulers and nobles. Then they went to the meeting. On gourd bases they set out different precious flowers. . . . And they carried golden necklaces, necklaces with pendants, wide necklaces.

And when Moctezuma went out to meet them, thereupon he gave various things to the war leader [Cortés]; he gave him flowers, he put necklaces on him, he put flower necklaces on him, he girded him with flowers, he put flower wreaths on his head. Then he laid before him the golden necklaces, all the different things for greeting people.

Then [Cortés] said in reply to Moctezuma "Is it not you? Is it not you then? Moctezuma?"

Moctezuma said, "Yes, it is me." Thereupon he stood up straight, he stood up with their faces meeting. He bowed down deeply to him. He stretched as far as he could, standing stiffly. Addressing him, he said to him:

"O our lord, be doubly welcomed on your arrival in this land; you have come to satisfy your curiosity about your altepetl of Mexico, you have come to sit on your seat of authority, which I have kept a while for you. . . . For a time I have been concerned, looking toward the mysterious place from which you have come, among clouds and mist. It is so that the [former] rulers on departing said that you would come in order to acquaint yourself with your altepetl and sit upon your seat of authority. And now it has come true, you have come."

[*Then Cortés responded:*] "Let Moctezuma be at ease, let him not be afraid, for we greatly esteem him. Now we are truly satisfied to see him in person and hear him, for until now we have greatly desired to see him and look upon his face. Well, now we have seen him, we have come to his homeland of Mexico. Bit by bit he will hear what we have to say."

Thereupon [the Spaniards] took [Moctezuma] by the hand. They came along with him, stroking his hair to show their good feeling. And the Spaniards looked at him, each of them giving him a close look. They would start along walking, then mount, then dismount again in order to see him.

Source: James Lockhart, ed. and trans., *We People Here: Nahuatl Accounts of the Conquest of Mexico* (Los Angeles: University of California Press, 1993), 108–18. Copyright 1993 by the Regents of the University of California. Reprinted by permission.

Source 13.3
Images of Encounter

Source 13.3A presents yet another Mesoamerican view of that epic encounter between Cortés and Moctezuma, drawn from the Lienzo de Tlaxcala, a series of paintings completed by 1560. Created by Tlaxcalan artists, who had absorbed some elements of European styles, these paintings highlighted the role of the Tlaxcalan people as valued allies of the Spanish.

Questions to consider as you examine the source:

■ How does this painting present the relationship between Cortés and Moctezuma? Are they meeting as equals, as enemies, as allies, or as ruler and subject? Notice that both sit on European-style chairs, which had come to suggest authority in the decades following Spanish conquest. Is it significant that Cortés is seated on a platform?

■ Does this image support or challenge the perception that the Aztecs viewed the Spanish newcomers, at least initially, in religious terms as gods?

■ What impression of Doña Marina does this image suggest?

Source 13.3A
Moctezuma and Cortés

Source 13.3B
The Massacre of the Nobles

Whatever the character of their initial meeting, the relationship of the Spanish and Aztecs soon deteriorated amid mutual suspicion. Within a week, Cortés had seized Moctezuma, holding him under a kind of house arrest in his own palaces. For reasons not entirely clear, this hostile act did not immediately trigger a violent Aztec response. Perhaps Aztec authorities were concerned for the life of their ruler, or possibly their factional divisions inhibited coordinated resistance.

But in May 1520, while Cortés was temporarily away at the coast, an incident occurred that set in motion the most violent phase of the encounter. During a religious ceremony in honor of Huitzilopochtli, the Aztec patron deity of Tenochtitlán, the local Spanish commander, apparently fearing an uprising, launched a surprise attack on the unarmed participants in the celebration, killing hundreds of the leading warriors and nobles. An Aztec account from *The Florentine Codex* described the scene:

> When the dance was loveliest and when song was linked to song, the Spaniards were seized with an urge to kill the celebrants. They all ran forward, armed as if for battle. They closed the entrances and passageways . . . then [they] rushed into the Sacred Patio to slaughter the inhabitants. . . . They attacked the man who was drumming and cut off his arms. Then they cut off his head, and it rolled across the floor. They attacked all the celebrants stabbing them, spearing them, striking them with swords. . . . Others they beheaded . . . or split their heads to pieces. . . . The blood of the warriors flowed like water and gathered into pools. . . . [T]hey invaded every room, hunting and killing."[1]

Source 13.3B shows a vivid Aztec depiction of this "massacre of the nobles," drawn from the *Codex Duran*, first published in 1581.

Questions to consider as you examine the source:

■ What elements of the preceding description are reflected in this painting?

■ What image of the Spanish does this painting reflect?

■ What do the drums in the center of the image represent?

The massacre of the nobles prompted a citywide uprising against the hated Spanish, who were forced to flee Tenochtitlán on June 30, 1520, across a causeway in Lake Texcoco amid ferocious fighting. Some six hundred Spaniards and several thousand of their Tlaxcalan allies perished in the escape, many of them laden with gold they had collected in Tenochtitlán. For the Spaniards, it was La Noche Triste (the night of sorrow), while for the Aztecs it was no doubt a fitting revenge and a great triumph.

Source 13.4
Conquest and Victory: The Fall of Tenochtitlán from a Spanish Perspective

While the Aztecs may well have thought themselves permanently rid of the Spanish, La Noche Triste offered only a temporary respite from the European invaders. Cortés and his now-diminished forces found refuge among their Tlaxcalan allies, where they regrouped and planned for yet another assault on Tenochtitlán. In mid-1521, Cortés returned, strengthened with yet more Mesoamerican allies, and laid siege to the Aztec capital. Bitter fighting ensued for several months, often in the form of house-to-house combat, ending with the surrender of the last Aztec emperor on August 13, 1521.

A Spanish account of this event comes from Francisco de Aguilar, a conquistador who took part in the siege of Tenochtitlán, though he subsequently regretted his action and became a priest. Much later in life, around 1560, he wrote an account of his experiences, including this description of the final battle of the Spanish conquest.

Questions to consider as you examine the source:

■ How does Aguilar account for the Spanish victory?

■ How does he portray the Spanish and their Aztec adversaries?

Francisco de Aguilar

Brief Record of the Conquest of New Spain

ca. 1560

[W]ith [Spanish] forces encircling the city and with the brigantines [warships], which were a great help on the lake, the city [Tenochtitlán] began to be battered by land and water. In addition great trouble was taken to cut off the fresh water from the springs, which reached the city by conduits. . . .

The Christians wounded some of the Indians, and great numbers of Indians were killed in the assaults on horseback and by the guns, harquebuses and crossbows. In spite of all this, they put up their strong barricades, and opened causeways and canals and defended themselves courageously. . . . They also killed some of the Spaniards and captured alive one of them called Guzman, who was Cortés's aide.

The war was sustained fiercely by both sides, since on our side we had the help of many Tlaxcalan warriors, while the Mexicans [had the advantage of] their rooftops and high buildings from which they battered us. . . . As soon as the Spaniards took any of the houses, which were all on the water, they had the Tlaxcalan Indians demolish and level them, for this gave more freedom to maneuver.

When some of the Indian lords inside the city began to see the danger they were in . . . , they decided to escape by night . . . [and] came over to our side. . . . In addition to this, when the Christians were exhausted from the war, God saw fit to send the Indians smallpox and there was a great pestilence in the city, because there were so many people there, especially women, and they had nothing more to eat. . . . Also for these reasons they began to slacken in their fighting.

The Mexicans, almost vanquished, withdrew to their fortresses on the water, and since a great number of women were left among them, they armed them all and stationed them on the rooftops. The Spaniards were alarmed at seeing so many of the enemy again, whooping and shouting at them, and when they began killing them and saw they were women, there was dismay on both sides.

[*Twice the last Aztec ruler, Cuauhtemoc, refused Spanish offers to surrender in return for a "pardon and many privileges." Then he was finally captured.*]

This done, the Spaniards seized the house that had been Cuauhtemoc's stronghold, where they found a great quantity of gold and jewels and other plunder. The Tlaxcalans, who were assisting us in the war . . . , knew [the city's] ins and outs, so that when they went home again, they were rich with the spoils they took.

Source: From *The Conquistadors: First-Person Accounts of the Conquest of Mexico*, edited by Patricia de Fuentes, translated by Patricia de Fuentes, translation copyright © 1963 by Penguin Random House LLC. Used by permission of Viking Books, an imprint of Penguin Publishing Group, a division of Penguin Random House LLC.

Source 13.5
Defeat: The Fall of Tenochtitlán from an Aztec Perspective

From *The Florentine Codex* (see Source 13.2) comes an Aztec account of what was to them a devastating defeat.

Questions to consider as you examine the source:

■ To what extent does this document confirm, contradict, or supplement Aguilar's account of the fall of Tenochtitlán?

■ How does this account explain the terrible defeat?

■ What posture toward the Spanish does this document reflect?

FRAY BERNARDINO DE SAHAGÚN
The Florentine Codex
Mid-Sixteenth Century

Before the Spaniards appeared to us, first an epidemic broke out, a sickness of pustules. . . . Large bumps spread on people; some were entirely covered. . . . [The disease] brought great desolation. . . . They could no longer walk about, but lay in their dwellings and sleeping places, no longer able to move or stir. . . . Very many people died of them; . . . starvation reigned, and no one took care of others any longer. . . . The Mexica warriors were greatly weakened by it.

And when things were in this state, the Spaniards came. . . . The warriors fought in boats; the warboat people shot at the Spaniards, and their arrows sprinkled down on them. . . . Many times they skirmished, and the Mexica went out to face them. . . .

When [the Spanish finished adjusting the guns], they shot at the wall. The wall then ripped and broke open. The second time it was hit, the wall went to the ground; it was knocked down in places, perforated, holes were blown in it. . . . [T]he warriors who had been lying at the wall dispersed and came fleeing; everyone escaped in fear. And then all the different people [who were on the side of the Spaniards] quickly went filling in the canals. . . . And when the canals were stopped up, some horse[men] came. . . . And the Spaniards did not move at all; when they fired the cannon, it grew very dark, and smoke spread. . . .

[In the fighting, the Aztecs captured fifty-three Spaniards and many of their allies.] Then [the Aztecs] took the captives. . . . Some went weeping, some singing, some went shouting while hitting their hands against their mouths. When they got to Yacacolco, they lined them all up. Each one went to the altar platform, where the sacrifice was performed. The Spaniards went first, going in the lead. . . . And when the sacrifice was over, they strung the Spaniards' heads on poles; they also strung up the horses' heads. . . .

And the common people suffered greatly. There was famine; many died of hunger. They no longer drank good, pure water, but the water they drank was salty. Many people died of it, and because of it many got dysentery and died. Everything was eaten: lizards, swallows, maize straw, grass that grows on salt flats. And they chewed at . . . wood, glue flowers, plaster, leather, and deerskin, which they roasted, baked and toasted so that they could eat them, and they ground up medicinal herbs and adobe bricks. There had never been the like of such suffering.

Along every stretch of road, the Spaniards took things from people by force. They were looking for gold; they cared nothing for green stone, feathers, or turquoise. They looked everywhere with the women, on their abdomens, under their skirts. And they looked everywhere with the men, under their loincloths and in their mouths. And [the Spaniards] took, picked out the beautiful women, with yellow bodies. And some of the women covered their faces with mud . . . , clothing themselves in rags. . . .

And when the weapons were laid down and we collapsed, the year was Three House and the day count was One Serpent.

Source: James Lockhart, ed. and trans., *We People Here: Nahuatl Accounts of the Conquest of Mexico* (Los Angeles: University of California Press, 1993), 108–18. Copyright 1993 by the Regents of the University of California. Reprinted by permission.

Source 13.6
The Battle of Tenochtitlán

The seizure of Tenochtitlán was a formative event in the creation of colonial Mexico and represented the starting point for the profound transformations to Mexican society that accompanied the conquest. In the centuries that followed, the drama of this event attracted the interest of artists, writers, and others in this new society. One particularly impressive late seventeenth-century effort to depict the siege was painted by an unknown artist in Mexico on a large folding screen most likely given by a local member of the Spanish elite to the new viceroy, Conde de Galve. On one side, the conquest of the city in 1521 unfolds in a series of scenes from the top left, where Cortés, bathed in sunshine, lands in Mexico and meets Moctezuma, to the bottom right, where in darker tones the Spanish are driven from the city on the "sad night" and Native American refugees flee into the surrounding forests to escape the violence. In between, scenes depicting critical moments in the conquest take place in different parts of an imagined cityscape. While key elements of the conquest story are present, the overall scene is most striking for its depiction of what one critic has called the "motley banquet of violence," which contrasts sharply with the serene, peaceful, and idealized cityscape of seventeenth-century Mexico City depicted on the other side of the screen.[2]

The scene reproduced here chronicles a dramatic moment from a central panel in the screen where Aztecs battle the Spanish near the Temple Mayor in the central plaza of Tenochtitlán. The building labeled D is the temple itself, depicted here as a hollowed-out octagon rather than in its true form, a towering pyramid. While violent scenes of battle swirl around the temple, in the background one can see the remains of ritually sacrificed Spanish soldiers and those of a horse, which had also been sacrificed.

Questions to consider as you examine the source:

■ What elements of the struggle described in Sources 13.4 and 13.5 can you identify?

■ Does this painting have a point of view? Was it created more from a European or an indigenous perspective?

■ Why might the artist have included the gruesome depiction of the executed Spaniards in this painting?

The Battle of Tenochtitlán

Museo Franz Mayer, Mexico City, Mexico/De Agostini Picture Library/Alfredo Dagli Orti/Bridgeman Images

Source 13.7
Lamentation: The Aftermath of Defeat

In the aftermath of this agonizing defeat, Aztec survivors composed a number of songs or poems, lamenting their terrible loss. These selections are part of a larger collection of Aztec poetry known as the *Cantares Mexicanos* (Songs of the Aztecs), compiled in the late sixteenth century.

Questions to consider as you examine the source:

■ What do the poems of lamentation suggest about Aztec efforts to come to terms with their enormous loss?

■ To what extent do these lamentations represent universal expressions of loss and defeat? In what ways might they be considered uniquely and distinctly Aztec?

Cantares Mexicanos
Late Sixteenth Century

The Fall of Tenochtitlán

Our cries of grief rise up / and our tears rain down, / for Tlatelolco [an Aztec city] is lost.

The Aztecs are fleeing across the lake; / they are running away like women.

How can we save our homes, my people? / The Aztecs are deserting the city:

the city is in flames, and all / is darkness and destruction . . .

Weep, my people: / know that with these disasters / we have lost the Mexican nation.

The water has turned bitter, / our food is bitter! / These are the acts of the Giver of Life . . .

The Aztecs are besieged in the city; / the Tlatelolcas are besieged in the city!

The walls are black, / the air is black with smoke, / the guns flash in the darkness.

They have captured Cuauhtemoc; / they have captured the princes of Mexico . . . /

The kings are prisoners now. / They are bound with chains.

Flowers and Songs of Sorrow

Nothing but flowers and songs of sorrow / are left in Mexico and Tlatelolco,

where once we saw warriors and wise men.

We know it is true / that we must perish, / for we are mortal men.

You, the Giver of Life, / you have ordained it.

We wander here / and there in our desolate poverty. / We are mortal men.

We have seen bloodshed and pain / where once we saw beauty and valor.

We are crushed to the ground; / we lie in ruins.

There is nothing but grief and suffering / In Mexico and Tlatelolco, /

where once we saw beauty and valor.

Have you grown weary of your servants? / Are you angry with your servants, / O Giver of Life?

Source: From *The Broken Spears* by Miguel León-Portilla. Copyright © 1962, 1990 by Miguel León-Portilla. Expanded and Updated Edition © 1992 by Miguel León-Portilla. Reprinted by permission of Beacon Press, Boston.

ESSAY QUESTIONS

The Spanish and the Aztecs: From Encounter to Conquest (1519–1521)

1. **Evaluating evidence and objectivity:** Based on these sources, how might a historian compose a history of the conquest of Mexico, seeking to be as objective as possible? What information from these sources might be reliably used, and what might be discarded? Is it in fact possible to be wholly objective about these events? How would such an account differ if it were written from a distinctly Aztec or Spanish point of view?

2. **Considering morality:** What moral or ethical issues arose for the participants in these events? Should historians take a position on such questions? Is it possible to avoid doing so?

3. **Considering outcomes:** Was Spanish victory inevitable? Under what circumstances might the outcome have been different?

4. **Assessing perspective:** What differences in outlook can you identify between the Spanish and the Aztec sources?

Notes

1. Stuart B. Schwartz, *Victors and Vanquished* (Boston: Bedford/St. Martin's, 2000), 164.

2. Much of this interpretation is taken from Anna More, *Baroque Sovereignty: Carlos de Sigüenza y Góngora and the Creole Archive of Colonial Mexico* (Philadelphia: University of Pennsylvania Press, 2012).

CHAPTER 14

THINKING THROUGH SOURCES

Voices from the Slave Trade

By any measure, the Atlantic slave trade was an enormous enterprise and enormously significant in modern world history: Its geographical scope encompassed four continents; it endured for almost four centuries; its victims numbered in the many millions; its commercial operation was global, complex, and highly competitive; and its consequences echo still in both public and private life. The sources that follow allow us to hear several individual voices from this vast historical process and to sample the evidence available to historians as they seek to chart this painful chapter of the human story.

Source 14.1
The Journey to Slavery

We begin with the voice of an individual victim of the slave trade — Olaudah Equiano. Born in what is now the Igbo-speaking region of southern Nigeria around 1745, Equiano was seized from his home at the age of eleven and sold into the Atlantic slave trade at the high point of that infamous commerce. In service to three different owners, his experience as a slave in the Americas was quite unusual. He learned to read and write, traveled extensively as a seaman aboard one of his masters' ships, and was allowed to buy his freedom in 1766. Settling in England, he became a prominent voice in the emerging abolitionist movement of the late eighteenth century and wrote a widely read account of his life, addressed largely to European Christians: "O, ye nominal Christians! Might not an African ask you, Learned you this from your God, who says unto you, Do unto all men as you would men should do unto you?" His book was published in 1789 as abolitionism was gaining wider acceptance.

Despite some controversy about his birthplace and birth date, most historians accept Equiano's autobiography as broadly accurate. Source 14.1 presents Equiano's account of his capture, his journey to the coast, his experience on a slave ship, and his arrival in the Americas. It was a journey forcibly undertaken by millions of others as well.

Questions to consider as you examine the source:

- How does Equiano describe the kind of slavery he knew in Africa? How does it compare with the plantation slavery of the Americas?

- What part did Africans play in the slave trade, according to this account?

- What aspects of the shipboard experience contributed to the slaves' despair?

OLAUDAH EQUIANO

The Interesting Narrative of the Life of Olaudah Equiano
1789

As we live in a country where nature is prodigal of her favours, our wants are few and easily supplied; of course we have few manufactures. They consist for the most part of calicoes, earthen ware, ornaments, and instruments of war and husbandry. . . . We have also markets, at which I have been frequently with my mother. These are sometimes visited by stout mahogany-coloured men from the south west of us: . . . They generally bring us fire-arms, gunpowder, hats, beads, and dried fish. . . . They always carry slaves through our land; . . . Sometimes indeed we sold slaves to them, but they were only prisoners of war, or such among us as had been convicted of kidnapping or adultery, and some other crimes, which we esteemed heinous. . . .

My father, besides many slaves, had a numerous family, of which seven lived to grow up, including myself and a sister, who was the only daughter. . . . I was trained up from my earliest years in the art of war; my daily exercise was shooting and throwing javelins; and my mother adorned me with emblems, after the manner of our greatest warriors. In this way I grew up till I was turned the age of eleven, when an end was put to my happiness in the following manner. . . .

One day, when all our people were gone out to their works as usual, and only I and my dear sister were left to mind the house, two men and a woman got over our walls and in a moment seized us both, and, without giving us time to cry out, or make resistance, they stopped our mouths, and ran off with us into the nearest wood. Here they tied our hands, and continued to carry us as far as they could, till night came on. . . . The next morning we left the house, and continued travelling all the day. For a long time we had kept [to] the woods, but at last we came into a road which I believed I knew. I had now some hopes of being delivered; for we had advanced but a little way before I discovered some people at a distance, on which I began to cry out for their assistance: but my cries had no other effect than to make them tie me faster and stop my mouth, and then they put me into a large sack. . . .

The next day proved a day of greater sorrow than I had yet experienced; for my sister and I were then separated, while we lay clasped in each other's arms. It was in vain that we besought them not to part us; she was torn from me, and immediately carried away. . . .

At length, after many days traveling, during which I had often changed masters, I got into the hands of a chieftain, in a very pleasant country. This man had two wives and some children, and they all used me extremely well, and did all they could to comfort me; particularly the first wife, who was something like my mother. Although I was a great many days journey from my father's house, yet these people spoke exactly the same language with us. . . .

[After about a month], I was again sold. . . . The people I was sold to used to carry me very often, when I was tired, either on their shoulders or on their backs. I saw many convenient well-built sheds along the roads, at proper distances, to accommodate the merchants and travelers, who lay in those buildings along with their wives, who often accompany them; and they always go well armed.

I was again sold, and carried through a number of places, till, after traveling a considerable time, I came to a town called Tinmah, in the most beautiful country I had yet seen in Africa. . . . Their money consisted of little white shells, the size of the finger nail. I was sold here for one hundred and seventy-two of them by a merchant who lived and brought me there. I had been about two or three days at his house, when a wealthy widow, a neighbor of his, came there one evening, and brought with her an only son, a young gentleman about my own age and size. Here they saw me; and, having taken a fancy to me, I was bought of the merchant, and went home with them. . . . The next day I was washed and perfumed, and when meal-time came I was led into the presence of my mistress, and ate and drank before her with her son. This filled me with astonishment; and I could scarce help expressing my surprise that the young gentleman should suffer me, who was bound, to eat with him who was free; and not only so, but that he would not at any time either eat or drink till I had taken first, because I was the eldest, which was agreeable to our custom. Indeed everything here, and all their treatment of me, made me forget that I was a slave. The language of these people resembled ours so nearly, that we understood each other perfectly. . . . In this resemblance to my former happy state I passed about two months; and I now began to think I was to be adopted into the family, and was beginning to be reconciled to my situation, and to forget by degrees my misfortunes when all at once the delusion vanished; for, without the least previous knowledge, one morning early, while my dear master and companion was still asleep, I was wakened out of my reverie to fresh sorrow, and hurried away. . . .

Thus I continued to travel, sometimes by land, sometimes by water, through different countries and various nations, till, at the end of six or seven months after I had been kidnapped, I arrived at the sea coast. . . . The first object which saluted my eyes when I arrived on the coast was the sea, and a slave ship, which was then riding at anchor, and waiting for its cargo. These filled me with astonishment, which was soon converted into terror when I was carried on board. I was immediately handled and tossed up to see if I were sound by some of the crew; and I was now persuaded that I had gotten into a world of bad spirits, and that they were going to kill me. Their complexions too differing so much from ours, their long hair, and the language they spoke . . . united to confirm me in this belief. . . . When I looked round the ship too and saw a large furnace or copper boiling, and a multitude of black people of every description chained together, every one of their countenances expressing dejection and sorrow, I no longer doubted of my fate; and quite overpowered with horror and anguish, I fell motionless on the deck and fainted. . . .

I was soon put down under the decks, and there I received such a salutation in my nostrils as I had never experienced in my life: so that, with the loathsomeness of the stench and crying together, I became so sick and low that I was not able to eat, nor had I the least desire to taste anything. I now wished for the last friend, death, to relieve me; but soon, to my grief, two of the white men offered me eatables; and on my refusing to eat, one of them held me fast by the hands, and laid me across I think the windlass and tied my feet, while the other flogged me severely. . . .

I had never seen among any people such instances of brutal cruelty; and this not only shewn towards us blacks, but also to some of the whites themselves. One white man in particular I saw, when we were permitted to be on deck, flogged so unmercifully with a large rope near the foremast that he died in consequence of it; and they tossed him over the side as they would have done a brute. . . .

The closeness of the place, and the heat of the climate, added to the number in the ship, which was so crowded that each had scarcely room to turn himself, almost suffocated us. This produced copious perspirations, so that the air soon became unfit for respiration, from a variety of loathsome smells, and brought on a sickness among the slaves, of which many died, thus falling victims to the improvident avarice, as I may call it, of their purchasers. This wretched situation was again aggravated by the galling of the chains, now become insupportable; and the filth of the necessary tubs, into which the children often fell, and were almost suffocated. The shrieks of the women, and the groans of the dying, rendered the whole a scene of horror almost inconceivable. . . .

At last we came in sight of the island of Barbados, at which the whites on board gave a great shout, and made many signs of joy to us. . . . Many merchants and planters now came on board, though it was in the evening. They put us in separate parcels, and examined us attentively. They also made us jump, and pointed to the land, signifying we were to go there. We thought by this we should be eaten by those ugly men, as they appeared to us; . . . at last the white people got some old slaves from the land to pacify us. They told us we were not to be eaten, but to work, and were soon to go on land, where we should see many of our country people. This report eased us much; and sure enough, soon after we were landed, there came to us Africans of all languages. We were conducted immediately to the merchant's yard, where we were all pent up together like so many sheep in a fold, without regard to sex or age.

Source: Olaudah Equiano, *The Interesting Narrative of the Life of Olaudah Equiano, or Gustavus Vassa, the African*, vol. 1 (London, 1789), chaps. 1, 2.

Source 14.2
The Business of the Slave Trade

For its African victims like Equiano, the slave trade was a horror beyond imagination; for kings and merchants — both European and African — it was a business. Source 14.2 shows how that business was conducted. It comes from the journal of an English merchant, Thomas Phillips, who undertook a voyage to the kingdom of Whydah in what is now the West African country of Benin in 1693–1694.

Questions to consider as you examine the source:

■ How would you describe the economic transactions described in the document? To what extent were they conducted between equal parties? Who, if anyone, held the upper hand in these dealings?

■ How might an African merchant have described the same transaction? How might Equiano have described it?

■ Notice the outcomes of Phillips's voyage to Barbados in the last two paragraphs. What does this tell you about European preferences for slaves, about the Middle Passage, and about the profitability of the enterprise?

Thomas Phillips

A Journal of a Voyage Made in the Hannibal *of London*

1694

As soon as the king understood of our landing, he sent two of his cappasheirs, or noblemen, to compliment us at our factory, where we design'd to continue that night, and pay our [respects] to his majesty next day . . . whereupon he sent two more of his grandees to invite us there that night, saying he waited for us, and that all former captains used to attend him the first night: whereupon being unwilling to infringe the custom, or give his majesty any offence, we took our hamocks, and Mr. Peirson, myself, Capt. Clay, our surgeons, pursers, and about 12 men, arm'd for our guard, were carry'd to the king's town, which contains about 50 houses. . . .

We returned him thanks by his interpreter, and assur'd him how great affection our masters, the royal African company of England, bore to him, for his civility and fair and just dealings with their captains; and that notwithstanding there were many other places, more plenty of negro slaves that begg'd their custom, yet they had rejected all the advantageous offers made them out of their good will to him, and therefore had sent us to trade with him, to support his country with necessaries, and that we hop'd he would endeavour to continue their favour by his kind usage and fair dealing with us in our trade, that we may have our slaves with all expedition. . . . He answer'd that we should be fairly dealt with, and not impos'd upon; But he did not prove as good as his word . . . so after having examin'd us about our cargoe, what sort of goods we had, and what quantity of slaves we wanted, etc., we took our leaves and return'd to the factory. . . .

According to promise we attended his majesty with samples of our goods, and made our agreement about the prices, tho' not without much difficulty; . . . next day we paid our customs to the king and cappasheirs, . . . then the bell was order'd to go about to give notice to all people to bring their slaves to the trunk to sell us. . . .

Capt. Clay and I had agreed to go to the trunk to buy the slaves by turns, each his day, that we might have no distractions or disagreement in our trade, as often happens when there are here more ships than one, and . . . their disagreements create animosities, underminings, and out-bidding each other, whereby they enhance the prices to their general loss and detriment, the blacks well knowing how to make the best use of such opportunities, and as we found make it their business, and endeavour to create and foment misunderstandings and jealousies between commanders, it turning to their great account in the disposal of their slaves.

When we were at the trunk, the king's slaves, if he had any, were the first offer'd to sale, . . . and we must not refuse them, tho' as I observ'd they were generally the worst slaves in the trunk, and we paid more for them than any others, which we could not remedy, it being one of his majesty's prerogatives: then the cappasheirs each brought out his slaves according to his degree and quality, the greatest first, etc. and our surgeon examin'd them well in all kinds, to see that they were sound wind and limb, making them jump, stretch out their arms swiftly, looking in their mouths to judge of their age; for the cappasheirs are so cunning, that they shave them all close before we see them, so that let them be never so old we can see no grey hairs in their heads or beards; and then having liquor'd them well and sleek with palm oil, 'tis no easy matter to know an old one from a middle-age one. . . .

When we had selected from the rest such as we liked, we agreed in what goods to pay for them, the prices being already stated before the king, how much of each sort of merchandize we were to give for a man, woman, and child, which gave us much ease, and saved abundance of disputes and wranglings. . . . [T]hen we mark'd the slaves we had bought in the breast, or shoulder, with a hot iron, having the letter of the ship's name on it, the place being before anointed with a little palm oil, which caus'd but little pain, the mark being usually well in four or five days, appearing very plain and white after. . . .

After we are come to an agreement for the prices of our slaves, . . . we are oblig'd to pay our customs to the king and cappasheirs for leave to trade, protection and justice; which for every ship are as follow, viz.

To the king six slaves value in cowries, or what other goods we can perswade him to take, but cowries are most esteem'd and desir'd; all which are measur'd in his presence, and he would wrangle with us stoutly about heaping up the measure.

To the cappasheirs in all two slaves value, as above. . . .

The best goods to purchase slaves here are cowries, the smaller the more esteem'd. . . .

The next in demand are brass neptunes or basons, very large, thin, and flat; for after they have bought them they cut them in pieces to make . . . bracelets, and collars for their arms legs and necks. . . .

[I]f they can discover that you have good store of cowries and brass aboard, then no other goods will serve their turn, till they have got as much as you have; and after, for the rest of the goods they will be indifferent, and make you come to their own terms, or else lie a long time for your slaves, so that those you have on board are dying while you are buying others ashore. . . .

Having bought my compliment of 700 slaves, viz. 480 men and 220 women, and finish'd all my business at Whidaw, I took my leave of the old king, and his cappasheirs, and parted, with many affectionate expressions on both sides, being forced to promise him that I would return again the next year, with several things he desired me to bring him from England; and having sign'd bills of lading . . . for the negroes aboard, I set sail the 27th of July in the morning. . . .

I deliver'd alive at Barbadoes to the company's factors 372, which being sold, came out at about nineteen pounds per head.

Source: Thomas Phillips, "A Journal of a Voyage Made in the *Hannibal* of London in 1694," in *Documents Illustrative of the History of the Slave Trade to America*, edited by Elizabeth Donnan (Washington, DC: Carnegie Institute, 1930), 399–405, 408, 410.

Source 14.3
The Slave Trade and the Kingdom of Kongo

While African elites often eagerly facilitated the traffic in slaves and benefited from doing so, in one well-known case, quite early in the slave-trade era, an African ruler sought to curtail it. This occurred in the Kingdom of Kongo, in what is now Angola. That state had welcomed Portuguese traders as early as the 1480s, for its rulers imagined that an alliance with Portugal could strengthen their regime. The royal family converted to Christianity and encouraged the importation of European guns, cattle, and horses. Several Kongolese were sent to Portugal for education, while Portuguese priests, artisans, merchants, and soldiers found a place in the kingdom. None of this worked as planned, however, and by the early sixteenth century, Kongo was in disarray and the authority of its ruler greatly undermined. This was the context in which its monarch Nzinga Mbemba, whose Christian name was Affonso I, wrote a series of letters to King João of Portugal in 1526, extracts of which are presented here.

Questions to consider as you examine the source:

■ What did Affonso seek from Portugal? What kind of relationship did he envisage with the Portuguese?

■ To what extent did Affonso seek the end of the slave trade? What was the basis for his opposition to it? Do you think he was opposed to slavery itself?

■ How did the operation of the slave trade in Kongo differ from that of Whydah as described in Source 14.2? How did the rulers of these two states differ in their relationship to Europeans?

KING AFFONSO I
Letters to King João of Portugal
1526

Sir, Your Highness [of Portugal] should know how our Kingdom is being lost in so many ways that it is convenient to provide for the necessary remedy, since this is caused by the excessive freedom given by your factors and officials to the men and merchants who are allowed to come to this Kingdom to set up shops with goods and many things which have been prohibited by us, and which they spread throughout our Kingdoms and Domains in such an abundance that many of our vassals, whom we had in obedience, do not comply because they have the things in greater abundance than we ourselves; and it was with these things that we had them content and subjected under our vassalage and jurisdiction, so it is doing a great harm not only to the service of God, but to the security and peace of our Kingdoms and State as well.

And we cannot reckon how great the damage is, since the mentioned merchants are taking every day our natives, sons of the land and the sons of our noblemen and vassals and our relatives, because the thieves and men of bad conscience grab them wishing to have the things and wares of this Kingdom which they are ambitious of; they grab them and get them to be sold; and so great, Sir, is the corruption and licentiousness that our country is being completely depopulated, and Your Highness should not agree with this nor accept it as in your service. And to avoid it we need from those [your] Kingdoms no more than some priests and a few people to teach in schools, and no other goods except wine and flour for the holy sacrament. That is why we beg of Your Highness to help and assist us in this matter, commanding your factors that they should not send here either merchants or wares, because it is our will that in these Kingdoms there should not be any trade of slaves nor outlet for them. Concerning what is referred above, again we beg of Your Highness to agree with it, since otherwise we cannot remedy such an obvious damage. . . .

Moreover, Sir, in our Kingdoms there is another great inconvenience which is of little service to God, and this is that many of our people, keenly desirous as they are of the wares and things of your Kingdoms, which are brought here by your people, and in order to satisfy their voracious appetite, seize many of our people, freed and exempt men; and very often it happens that they kidnap even noblemen and the sons of noblemen, and our relatives, and take them to be sold to the white men who are in our Kingdoms; and for this purpose they have concealed them; and others are brought during the night so that they might not be recognized.

And as soon as they are taken by the white men they are immediately ironed and branded with fire, and when they are carried to be embarked, if they are caught by our guards' men the whites allege that they have bought them but they cannot say from whom, so that it is our duty to do justice and to restore to the freemen their freedom, but it cannot be done if your subjects feel offended, as they claim to be.

And to avoid such a great evil we passed a law so that any white man living in our Kingdoms and wanting to purchase goods in any way should first inform three of our noblemen and officials of our court . . . who should investigate if the mentioned goods are captives or free men, and if cleared by them there will be no further doubt nor embargo for them to be taken and embarked. But if the white men do not comply with it they will lose the aforementioned goods. . . .

Sir, Your Highness has been kind enough to write to us saying that we should ask in our letters for anything we need, and that we shall be provided with everything, and as the peace and the health of our Kingdom depend on us, and as there are among us old folks and people who have lived for many days, it happens that we have continuously many and different diseases which put us very often in such a weakness that we reach almost the last extreme; and the same happens to our children, relatives, and natives owing to the lack in this country of physicians and surgeons who might know how to cure properly such diseases. And as we have got neither dispensaries nor drugs which might help us in this forlornness, many of those who had been already confirmed and instructed in the holy faith of Our Lord Jesus Christ perish and die; and the rest of the people in their majority cure themselves with herbs and breads and other ancient methods, so that they put all their faith in the mentioned herbs and ceremonies if they live, and believe that they are saved if they die; and this is not much in the service of God.

And to avoid such a great error and inconvenience, since it is from God in the first place and then from your Kingdoms and from Your Highness that all the goods and drugs and medicines have come to save us, we beg of you to be agreeable and kind enough to send us two physicians and two apothecaries and one surgeon, so that they may come with their drugstores and all the necessary things to stay in our kingdoms, because we are in extreme need of them all and each of them.

Source: Basil Davidson, *The African Past* (Boston: Little, Brown, 1964), 191–94.

Source 14.4
The Slave Trade and the Kingdom of Asante

The slave trade did not always have such politically destabilizing effects as it did in Kongo. In the region known as the Gold Coast (now the modern state of Ghana), the Kingdom of Asante (uh-SAWN-tay) arose in the eighteenth century, occupying perhaps 100,000 square miles and incorporating some 3 million people. It was a powerful conquest state, heavily invested in the slave trade, from which much of its wealth derived. Many slaves from its wars of expansion and from the tribute of its subject people were funneled into Atlantic commerce, while still others were used as labor in the gold mines and on the plantations within Asante itself. No wonder, then, that the ruler (or Asantehene) Osei Bonsu was dismayed in the early nineteenth century when, in reaction to the expanding abolitionist movement, the British stopped buying slaves. A conversation between Osei Bonsu and a British diplomat in 1820 highlights the role of the slave trade in Asante and in the thinking of its monarch.

Questions to consider as you examine the source:

■ How did Osei Bonsu understand the slave trade and its significance for his kingdom?

■ Some scholars have argued that the slave trade increased the incidence of warfare in West Africa as various states deliberately sought captives whom they could exchange for desired goods from Europe. How might Osei Bonsu respond to that idea? What was his understanding of the relationship between war and the slave trade?

■ In what ways did Osei Bonsu compare Muslim traders from the north with European merchants from the sea?

OSEI BONSU

Conversation with Joseph Dupuis

1820

"Now," said the king, after a pause, "I have another palaver, and you must help me to talk it. A long time ago the great king [of England] liked plenty of trade, more than now; then many ships came, and they bought ivory, gold, and slaves; but now he will not let the ships come as before, and the people buy gold and ivory only. This is what I have in my head, so now tell me truly, like a friend, why does the king do so?" "His majesty's question," I replied, "was connected with a great palaver, which my instructions did not authorise me to discuss. I had nothing to say regarding the slave trade." "I know that too," retorted the king; "because, if my master liked that trade, you would have told me so before. I only want to hear what you think as a friend: this is not like the other palavers." I was confessedly at a loss for an argument that might pass as a satisfactory reason, and the sequel proved that my doubts were not groundless. The king did not deem it plausible, that this obnoxious traffic should have been abolished from motives of humanity alone; neither would he admit that it lessened the number either of domestic or foreign wars.

Taking up one of my observations, he remarked, "[T]he white men who go to council with your master, and pray to the great God for him, do not understand my country, or they would not say the slave trade was bad. But if they think it bad now, why did they think it good before? Is not your law an old law, the same as the Crammo [Muslim] law? Do you not both serve the same God, only you have different fashions and customs? Crammos are strong people in fetische [magical powers], and they say the law is good, because the great God made the book [Quran]; so they buy slaves, and teach them good things, which they knew not before. This makes everybody love the Crammos, and they go everywhere up and down, and the people give them food when they want it. Then these men come all the way from the great water [Niger River], and from Manding, and Dagomba, and Killinga; they stop and trade for slaves, and then go home. If the great king would like to restore this trade, it would be good for the white men and for me too, because Ashantee is a country for war, and the people are strong; so if you talk that palaver for me properly, in the white country, if you go there, I will give you plenty of gold, and I will make you richer than all the white men."

I urged the impossibility of the king's request, promising, however, to record his sentiments faithfully. "Well then," said the king, "you must put down in my master's book all I shall say, and then he will look to it, now he is my friend. And when he sees what is true, he will surely restore that trade. I cannot make war to catch slaves in the bush, like a thief. My ancestors never did so. But if I fight a king, and kill him when he is insolent, then certainly I must have his gold, and his slaves, and the people are mine too. Do not the white kings act like this? Because I hear the old men say, that before I conquered Fantee and killed the Braffoes and the kings, that white men came in great ships, and fought and killed many people; and then they took the gold and slaves to the white country: and sometimes they fought together. That is all the same as these black countries. The great God and the fetische made war for strong men every where, because then they can pay plenty of gold and proper sacrifice. When I fought Gaman, I did not make war for slaves, but because Dinkera (the king) sent me an arrogant message and killed my people, and refused to pay me gold as his father did. Then my fetische made me strong like my ancestors, and I killed Dinkera, and took his gold, and brought more than 20,000 slaves to Coomassy. Some of these people being bad men, I washed my stool in their blood for the fetische. But then some were good people, and these I sold or gave to my captains: many, moreover, died, because this country does not grow too much corn like Sarem, and what can I do? Unless I kill or sell them, they will grow strong and kill my people. Now you must tell my master that these slaves can work for him, and if he wants 10,000 he can have them. And if he wants fine handsome girls and women to give his captains, I can send him great numbers."

Source: Joseph Dupuis, *Journal of a Residence in Ashantee* (London: Henry Colburn, 1824), 162–64.

Source 14.5
Images of the Slave Trade

Images of the slave trade abound, offering another perspective on the journey from freedom to slavery. Source 14.5A, a French engraving published in 1796 as part of an encyclopedic travel book, shows the sale of slaves at Gorée, a major slave-trading port in what is now Dakar in Senegal. A European merchant and an African slave trader negotiate the arrangement, while the shackled victims wait for their fate to be decided. Based on an early photograph, Source 14.5B is an engraving published in the popular American periodical *Harper's Weekly* in 1860. It illustrates the Middle Passage by recording the enormously crowded conditions aboard a slave ship, which was captured before it could land its human cargo in Cuba. And Source 14.5C, a handbill advertising a slave auction in South Carolina in 1769, indicates what lay ahead for those who survived the Middle Passage.

Questions to consider as you examine the sources:

■ What aspects of the documents in Sources 14.1 through 14.4 do these images illustrate?

■ In what ways do images such as these provide an understanding of the slave trade beyond what written sources can convey? And what are their limitations as sources useful to historians?

Source 14.5A
Sale of Slaves in West Africa

Slave Merchant in Gorée Island, Senegal, from *Encyclopédie des Voyages*, engraved by L. F. Labrousse, 1796/Bibliothèque des Arts Décoratifs, Paris, France/Archives Charmet/Bridgeman Images

Source 14.5B
The Slave Ship Wildfire

THE SLAVE DECK OF THE BARK "WILDFIRE," BROUGHT INTO KEY WEST ON APRIL 30, 1860.—[FROM A DAGUERREOTYPE.]

Source 14.5C
Advertisement for a Slave Auction in Charleston, SC

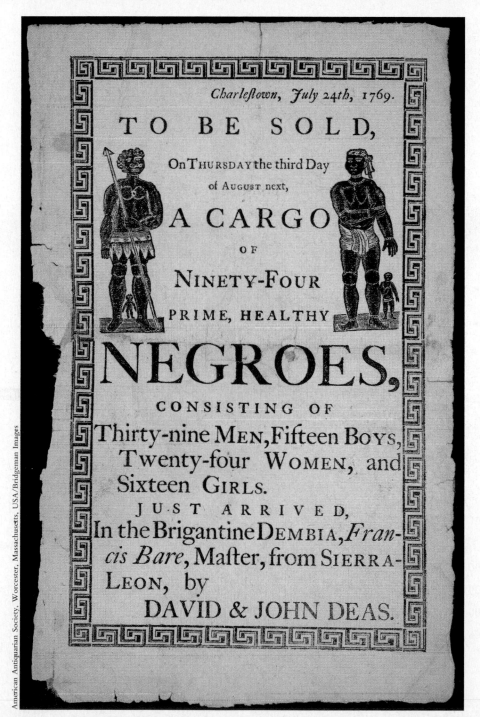

Source 14.6
Data: Patterns of the Slave Trade

Numbers, or quantitative data, may not convey the same immediacy or emotional impact that images or first-person accounts often carry. But they have a role in historians' efforts to understand the slave trade. Here are two tables and an aggregate statistic that provide information on various aspects of the slave trade. They are derived from the Trans-Atlantic Slave Trade Database (slavevoyages.org), a huge collection of searchable information culled from almost 35,000 individual slave voyages.

Questions to consider as you examine the sources:

■ What kind of understandings can be obtained from data such as this that are not available from the other sources in this feature? What are the limitations of this information?

■ In what ways did the slave trade change over time, according to this data? How might you account for these changes?

■ What might you find surprising in this data?

Source 14.6A
Voyages and Slave Rebellion: An Aggregate Statistic

Overall percentage of voyages (1501–1866) that experienced a major slave rebellion:

10 percent

Source 14.6B
Changing Patterns of the Slave Trade

Century	Total Taken from Africa	Total Landed at Destination	% Died During Middle Passage	Avg. Days in Middle Passage	Avg. % Slaves = Children	Avg. % Slaves = Male
1501–1600	227,506	199,285	12.0	—	0	58
1601–1700	1,875,631	1,522,677	23.3	76.1	11.6	58.4
1701–1800	6,494,619	5,609,869	11.9	70	18.4	64.2
1801–1866	3,873,580	3,370,825	10.3	45.9	29.4	67.6
Total or Average	12,521,336 (Total)	10,702,656 (Total)	11.9 (Avg.)	60 (Avg.)	20.9 (Avg.)	64.7 (Avg.)

Source: Voyages Database. 2009. *Voyagtes: The Trans-Atlantic Slave Trade Database.* http://www.slavevoyages.org (accessed June 8, 2015).

Source 14.6C
Percentage of Slave Arrivals by Destination

Century	Europe	North America	Caribbean	Spanish American Mainland	Brazil	Africa	Other
1501–1600	1.1	—	8	66.7	1.9	0.3	22
1601–1700	0.6	1.5	56.4	22.7	17	0.1	1.6
1701–1800	0.1	5.2	64.4	1.2	29	0.1	0.1
1801–1866	—	2.0	31.9	0.9	60	4.8	0
Average of Total	0.1	3.8	51.9	3.3	38.9	1.8	0.3

Source: Voyages Database. 2009. *Voyages: The Trans-Atlantic Slave Trade Database.* http://www.slavevoyages.org (accessed June 8, 2015).

ESSAY QUESTIONS

Voices from the Slave Trade

1. **Noticing what's missing:** What perspectives are missing that might add other dimensions to our understanding of this commerce in people?

2. **Integrating sources and the text narrative:** In what ways do these sources support, illustrate, supplement, or contradict this chapter's narrative discussion of the slave trade?

3. **Assessing historical responsibility:** What light do these documents shed on the much-debated question about who should be held responsible for the tragedy of the Atlantic slave trade?

CHAPTER 15

Renewal and Reform in the Early Modern World

Cultural and religious traditions change over time in various ways and for various reasons. Some of these changes occur as a result of internal tensions or criticisms within these traditions or in response to social and economic transformations in the larger society. The Protestant Reformation, for example, grew out of deep dissatisfaction with the prevailing teachings and practices of the Roman Catholic Church and drew support from a growing middle class and a disaffected peasantry. At other times, cultural change occurred by incorporating or reacting against new ideas drawn from contact with outsiders. Chinese Confucianism took on a distinctive tone and flavor as it drew on the insights of Buddhism, and a new South Asian religion called Sikhism sought to combine elements of Hindu and Muslim beliefs. Whatever the stimulus for cultural change, departures from accepted ways of thinking have sometimes been expressed as a return to a purer and more authentic past, even if that past is largely imaginary. In other cases, however, change was presented as a necessary break from an outmoded past even if many elements from earlier times were retained.

All across the Eurasian world of the early modern era — in Western Europe, India, and the Middle East — significant protests against established ways of thinking were brewing. In each of the sources that follow, we are listening in on just one side of extended debates or controversies, focusing on those seeking change. To what extent were these changes moving in the same direction? How did they differ? What were the sources of these changes, and how were they expressed? How might those who opposed these changes respond?

Source 15.1
Luther's Protest

Europe was home to perhaps the most substantial cultural transformations of the early modern centuries. There the Protestant Reformation sharply challenged both the doctrines and the authority of the Roman Catholic Church, ending the religious monopoly that the church had exercised in Western Europe for many centuries and introducing a bitter and often-violent divide into the religious and political life of the region. Then the practitioners of the Scientific Revolution, and the Enlightenment that followed from it, introduced a revolutionary new understanding of both the physical world and human society while urging novel means of obtaining knowledge.

The Protestant Reformation and the Scientific Revolution/Enlightenment shared a common hostility to established authority, and they both represented a clear departure from previous patterns of thought and behavior. But they differed sharply in how they represented the changes they sought. Reformation leaders looked to the past, seeking to restore or renew what they believed was an earlier and more authentic version of Christianity. Leaders of the Scientific Revolution and the Enlightenment, on the other hand, foresaw and embraced an altogether new world in the making. They were the "moderns" combating the "ancients."

The most prominent figure in the Protestant Reformation was Martin Luther (1483–1546), a German monk, priest, and theologian. A prolific writer, Luther composed theological treatises, translations of the Bible into German, and many hymns. The excerpts in Source 15.1, however, come from conversations with his students, friends, and colleagues, which they carefully recorded. After Luther's death, these recollections of the reformer's thoughts were compiled and published under the title *Table Talk*.

Questions to consider as you examine the source:

■ Based on this source, what issues drove the Protestant Reformation?

■ What theological questions are addressed in these excerpts? How does Luther understand the concepts of law, good works, grace, and faith?

■ In what ways is Luther critical of the papacy, monks, and the monastic orders of the Catholic Church?

MARTIN LUTHER

Table Talk

Early Sixteenth Century

On the Bible

No greater mischief can happen to a Christian people, than to have God's Word taken from them, or falsified, so that they no longer have it pure and clear. The ungodly papists prefer the authority of the church far above God's Word; a blasphemy abominable and not to be endured; wherewith, void of all shame and piety, they spit in God's face.

Pope, cardinals, bishops, not a soul of them has read the Bible; 'tis a book unknown to them. They are a pack of guzzling, stuffing wretches, rich, wallowing in wealth and laziness, resting secure in their power, and never, for a moment, thinking of accomplishing God's will.

On Salvation

He that goes from the gospel to the law, thinking to be saved by good works, falls as uneasily as he who falls from the true service of God to idolatry; for, without Christ, all is idolatry and fictitious imaginings of God, whether of the Turkish Koran [Quran], of the pope's decrees, or Moses' law.

The Gospel preaches nothing of the merit of works; he that says the Gospel requires works for salvation, I say, flat and plain, is a liar. Nothing that is properly good proceeds out of the works of the law, unless grace be present; for what we are forced to do, goes not from the heart, nor is acceptable.

But a true Christian says: I am justified and saved only by faith in Christ, without any works or merits of my own. . . .

Prayer in popedom is mere tongue-threshing . . . ; not prayer but a work of obedience.

On the Pope and the Church Hierarchy

The great prelates, the puffed-up saints, the rich usurers, the ox drovers that seek unconscionable gain, etc., these are not God's servants. . . .

Our dealing and proceeding against the pope is altogether excommunication, which is simply the public declaration that a person is disobedient to Christ's Word. Now we affirm in public, that the pope and his retinue believe not; therefore we conclude that he shall not be saved, but be damned. . . .

Antichrist is the pope and the Turk together; a beast full of life must have a body and soul; the spirit or soul of antichrist is the pope, his flesh or body the Turk. . . . Kings and princes coin money

only out of metals, but the pope coins money out of every thing — indulgences, ceremonies, dispensations, pardons; 'tis all fish comes to his net. . . .

The pope and his crew are mere worshippers of idols, and servants of the devil. . . . He pretends great holiness, under color of the outward service of God, for he has instituted orders with hoods, with shavings, fasting, eating of fish, saying mass, and such like. . . . [F]or his doctrine he gets money and wealth, honor and power, and is so great a monarch, that he can bring emperors under his girdle.

The chief cause that I fell out with the pope was this: the pope boasted that he was the head of the church, and condemned all that would not be under his power and authority. . . .

The fasting of the friars is more easy to them than our eating to us. For one day of fasting there are three of feasting. Every friar for his supper has two quarts of beer, a quart of wine, and spice-cakes, or bread prepared with spice and salt, the better to relish their drink. Thus go on these poor fasting brethren; getting so pale and wan, they are like the fiery angels.

The state of celibacy is great hypocrisy and wickedness. . . . Christ with one sentence confutes all their arguments: God created them male and female. . . . Now eating, drinking, marrying, etc., are of God's making, therefore they are good. . . .

A Christian's worshipping is not the external, hypocritical mask that our spiritual friars wear, when they chastise their bodies, torment and make themselves faint, with ostentatious fasting, watching, singing, wearing hair shirts, scourging themselves, etc. Such worshipping God desires not.

Source: William Hazlitt, ed. and trans., *The Table Talk of Martin Luther* (London: H. G. Bohn, 1857).

Source 15.2
Calvinism and Catholicism

Protestant opposition to Roman Catholic practice was not limited to matters of theology, liturgy, and church corruption, but came to include as well the physical appearance of churches. Martin Luther was suspicious of the many sculptures and paintings that served as objects of devotion to the Catholic faithful, but John Calvin, the prominent French-born Protestant theologian went even further, declaring that "God forbade . . . the making of any images representing him."

Perhaps the most dramatic expression of these ideas took place in regions of Europe where Protestants took over formerly Roman Catholic churches for their new forms of worship. During the 1560s, waves of Protestant image smashing, sometimes called the Iconoclastic Fury, took place in England, France, Switzerland, the Netherlands, and elsewhere. This engraving, produced in 1566 at the height of these religious conflicts, depicts Protestants "cleansing" a Catholic church in Antwerp in what is now Belgium of what they viewed as idolatrous decorations but Catholics revered as objects of devotion.

An English Catholic observer described this event and others like it with horror: "These fresh followers of this new preaching [Protestantism] threw down the graven and defaced the painted images. . . . They tore the curtains, dashed in pieces the carved work of brass and stone, . . . pulled up the brass of the gravestones. . . . [T]he Blessed Sacrament of the altar . . . they trod under their feet and (horrible it is to say!) shed their stinking piss upon it. . . . [T]hese false brethren burned and rent not only all kind of Church books, but, moreover, destroyed whole libraries of books of all sciences and tongues, yea the Holy Scriptures and the ancient fathers, and tore in pieces the maps and charts of the descriptions of countries."[1]

These often-dramatic attacks on churches served a practical purpose in preparing the site for Protestant worship. But they also reflected the new beliefs of the Protestants, or, as one scholar has put it, expressed "theology in stone." These churches were stripped of visual distractions and altars where the miracle of the mass took place. Instead there emerged a church, frequently without any images or other diversions like organs or other musical instruments, whose main focal point was the pulpit where the word of God was preached.

Questions to consider as you examine the source:

■ What elements of the Catholic description of this attack can you identify in the image? What other acts of destruction can you notice?

■ What differences in religious understanding lay behind such attacks?

■ What accounts for the passion displayed in these attacks? Is this kind of religious violence a thing of the past or does it have contemporary counterparts today?

Calvinists Destroying Statues in a Catholic Church
·1566·

Source 15.3
Progress and Enlightenment

If the Protestant Reformation represented a major change within the frame-work of the Christian faith, the Scientific Revolution and the European Enlightenment came to be seen by many as a challenge to all Christian understandings of the world. After all, these two movements celebrated the powers of human reason to unlock the mysteries of the universe and proclaimed the possibility of a new human society shaped by human rea-son. Among the most prominent spokesmen for the Enlightenment was the Marquis de Condorcet (1743–1794), a French mathematician, philosopher, and active participant in the French Revolution. In his *Sketch of the Progress of the Human Mind*, Condorcet described ten stages of human development. Source 15.3 contains excerpts from "The Ninth Epoch," whose title refers to the era in which Condorcet was living, and the "The Tenth Epoch," referring to the age to come. Condorcet's optimism about that future was not borne out in his own life, for he fell afoul of the radicalism of the French Revolution and died in prison in 1794.

Questions to consider as you examine the source:

■ What is Condorcet's view of the relationship between the Scientific Revolution and the Enlightenment?

■ How, precisely, does Condorcet imagine the future of humankind?

■ How might Martin Luther respond to Condorcet's vision of the future? How do their understandings of human potential differ?

MARQUIS DE CONDORCET
Sketch of the Progress of the Human Mind
1793–1794

The Ninth Epoch: From Descartes to the Formation of the French Republic

[T]he progress of philosophy . . . destroyed within the general mass of people the prejudices that have afflicted and corrupted the human race for so long a time.

Humanity was finally permitted to boldly proclaim the long ignored right to submit every opinion to reason, that is to utilize the only instru-ment given to us for grasping and recognizing the truth. Each human learned with a sort of pride

that nature had never destined him to believe the word of others. The superstitions of antiquity and the abasement of reason before the madness of supernatural religion disappeared from society just as they had disappeared from philosophy. . . .

If we were to limit ourselves to showing the benefits derived from the immediate applications of the sciences, or in their applications to man-made devices for the well-being of individuals and the prosperity of nations, we would be making known only a slim part of their benefits. The most important, perhaps, is having destroyed prejudices, and reestablished human intelligence, which until then had been forced to bend down to false instructions instilled in it by absurd beliefs passed on to the children of each generation by the terrors of superstition and the fear of tyranny. . . .

The advances of scientific knowledge are all the more deadly to these errors because they destroy them without appearing to attack them, while lavishing on those who stubbornly defend them the degrading taunt of ignorance. . . .

Finally this progress of scientific knowledge . . . results in a belief that not birth, professional status, or social standing gives anyone the right to judge something he does not understand. This unstoppable progress cannot be observed without having enlightened men search unceasingly for ways to make the other branches of learning follow the same path. . . .

The Tenth Epoch: The Future Progress of the Human Mind

Our hopes for the future of the human species may be reduced to three important points: the destruction of inequality among nations; the progress of equality within nations themselves; and finally, the real improvement of humanity. Should not all the nations of the world approach one day the state of civilization reached by the most enlightened peoples such as the French and the Anglo-Americans? Will not the slavery of nations subjected to kings, the barbarity of African tribes, and the ignorance of savages gradually disappear? . . .

If we cast an eye at the existing state of the globe, we will see right away that in Europe the principles of the French constitution are already those of all enlightened men. We will see that they are too widely disseminated and too openly professed for the efforts of tyrants and priests to prevent them from penetrating into the hovels of their slaves. . . .

Can it be doubted that either wisdom or the senseless feuds of the European nations themselves, working with the slow but certain effects of progress in their colonies, will not soon produce the independence of the new world; and that then the European population, spreading rapidly across that immense land, must either civilize or make disappear the savage peoples that now inhabit these vast continents? . . .

Thus the day will come when the sun will shine only on free men born knowing no other master but their reason; where tyrants and their slaves, priests and their ignorant, hypocritical writings will exist only in the history books and theaters. . . . If we consider the human creations based on scientific theories, we shall see that their progress can have no limits; . . . that new tools, machines, and looms will add every day to the capabilities and skill of humans; they will improve and perfect the precision of their products while decreasing the amount of time and labor needed to produce them. . . .

A smaller piece of land will be able to produce commodities of greater usefulness and value than before; greater benefits will be obtained with less waste; the production of the same industrial product will result in less destruction of raw materials and greater durability. . . . [E]ach individual will work less but more productively and will be able to better satisfy his needs. . . .

Among the advances of the human mind we should reckon as most important for the general welfare is the complete destruction of those prejudices that have established an inequality of rights between the sexes, an inequality damaging even to the party it favors. . . .

The most enlightened people . . . will slowly come to perceive war as the deadliest plague and the most monstrous of crimes. . . . They will understand that they cannot become conquerors without losing their liberty; that perpetual alliances are the only way to preserve independence; and that they should seek their security, not power. . . .

We may conclude then that the perfectibility of humanity is indefinite.

Finally, can we not also extend the same hopes to the intellectual and moral faculties? . . . Is it not also probable that education, while perfecting these qualities, will also influence, modify, and improve that bodily nature itself? . . .

Source: Marquis de Condorcet, *Sketch of the Progress of the Human Mind* (Paris: Firmin Didot Frères, 1847), Epoch 9 and Epoch 10.

Source 15.4
Art and Enlightenment

Public lectures on scientific topics became widespread in Europe during the eighteenth century, serving to spread the new knowledge and to bring "enlightenment" to a wider circle of people. The following painting, titled *A Philosopher Giving a Lecture on the Orrery*, by English artist Joseph Wright (1734–1797), illustrates such a presentation. The central figure in a red robe, modeled, some suggest, on the famous scientist Isaac Newton, is demonstrating the movements of the planets around the sun, using an "orrery," a mechanical device that shows their orbits and their relationship to one another. His captivated audience includes three men, two small boys, and two girls or young women. The light source is an oil lamp, which represents the sun at the center of the solar system.

Questions to consider as you examine the source:

■ The kind of fascination or awe that characterizes the spectators had previously been reserved largely for witnesses to religious events. What is stimulating that sense of wonderment in this painting? Is there something quasi-religious about the scene?

■ What metaphorical or symbolic meaning might be attached to the illuminated faces, which contrast sharply with the surrounding darkness?

■ In what ways does this painting illustrate Condorcet's vision of the role that science and reason will play in the coming age of progress and enlightenment?

JOSEPH WRIGHT
A Philosopher Giving a Lecture on the Orrery

The Orrery (ca. 1766) by Joseph Wright of Derby (1734–1797)/Derby Museum and Art Gallery, UK/Bridgeman Images

Source 15.5
The Wahhabi Perspective on Islam

Within the Islamic world, the major cultural movements of the early modern era were those of religious renewal. Such movements sought to eliminate the "deviations" that had crept into Islamic practice over the centuries and to return to a purer version of the faith that presumably had prevailed during the foundational period of the religion. The most influential of these movements was associated with Muhammad Ibn Abd al-Wahhab, whose revivalist movement spread widely in Arabia during the second half of the eighteenth century. Source 15.5, written by the grandson of al-Wahhab shortly after the capture of Mecca in 1803, provides a window into the outlook of Wahhabi Islam.

Questions to consider as you examine the source:

- What specific objections did the Wahhabis have to the prevailing practice of Islam in eighteenth-century Arabia?

- How did the Wahhabis put their ideas into practice once they had seized control of Mecca?

- What similarities do you see between the outlook of the Wahhabis and that of Martin Luther? What differences can you identify?

ABDULLAH WAHHAB

History and Doctrines of the Wahhabis

1803

Now I was engaged in the holy war . . . , when God, praised be He, graciously permitted us to enter Mecca. . . . Now, though we were more numerous, better armed and disciplined than the people of Mecca, yet we did not cut down their trees, neither did we hunt, nor shed any blood except the blood of victims, and of those four-footed beasts which the Lord has made lawful by his commands.

When our pilgrimage was over . . . our leader, whom the Lord saves, explained to the divines what we required of the people, . . . namely, a pure belief in the Unity of God Almighty. He pointed out to them that there was no dispute between us and them except on two points, and that one of these was a sincere belief in the Unity of God, and a knowledge of the different kinds of prayer. . . .

They then acknowledged our belief, and there was not one among them who doubted. . . . And they swore a binding oath, although we had not asked them, that their hearts had been opened and their doubts removed, and that they were convinced whoever said, "Oh prophet of God!" or "Oh Ibn 'Abbes!" or "Oh 'Abdul Qadir!" or called on any other created being, thus entreating him to turn away evil or grant what is good (where the power belongs to God alone), such as recovery from sickness, or victory over enemies, or protection from temptation, etc.; he is a Mushrik, guilty of the most heinous form of shirk [unbelief], his blood shall be shed and property confiscated. . . . Again, the tombs which had been erected over the remains of the pious, had become in these times as it were idols where the people went to pray for what they required; they humbled themselves before them, and called upon those lying in them, in their distress, just as did those who were in darkness before the coming of Muhammad. . . .

We razed all the large tombs in the city which the people generally worshipped and believed in, and by which they hoped to obtain benefits or ward off evil, so that there did not remain an idol to be adored in that pure city, for which God be praised. Then the taxes and customs we abolished, all the different kinds of instruments for using tobacco we destroyed, and tobacco itself we proclaimed forbidden. Next we burned the dwellings of those selling hashish, and living in open wickedness, and issued a proclamation, directing the people to constantly exercise themselves in prayer. They were not to pray in separate groups . . . , but all were directed to arrange themselves at each time of prayer behind any Imam who is a follower of any of the four Imams [founders of major schools of Islamic law]. . . . For in this way the Lord would be worshiped by as it were one voice, the faithful of all sects would become friendly disposed towards each other, and all dissensions would cease. . . .

[W]e do not reject anyone who follows any of the four Imams, as do the Shias. . . . We do not claim to exercise our reason in all matters of religion, and of our faith, save that we follow our judgment where a point is clearly demonstrated to us in either the Quran or the Sunnah [traditions of Muhammad's actions]. . . . We do not command the destruction of any writings except such as tend to cast people into infidelity to injure their faith, such as those on Logic, which have been prohibited by all Divines. But we are not very exacting with regard to books or documents of this nature; if they appear to assist our opponents, we destroy them. . . . We do not consider it proper to make Arabs prisoners of war, nor have we done so, neither do we fight with other nations. Finally, we do not consider it lawful to kill women or children. . . .

We consider pilgrimage is supported by legal custom, but it should not be undertaken except to a mosque, and for the purpose of praying in it. Therefore, whoever performs pilgrimage for this purpose, is not wrong, and doubtless those who spend the precious moments of their existence in invoking the Prophet, shall . . . obtain happiness in this world and the next. . . . We do not deny miraculous powers to the saints, but on the contrary allow them. . . . But whether alive or dead, they must not be made the object of any form of worship. . . .

We prohibit those forms of Bidah [innovation or heresy] that affect religion or pious works. Thus drinking coffee, reciting poetry, praising kings, do not affect religion or pious works and are not prohibited. . . .

All games are lawful. Our prophet allowed play in his mosque. So it is lawful to chide and punish persons in various ways; to train them in the use of different weapons; or to use anything which tends to encourage warriors in battle, such as a war-drum. But it must not be accompanied with musical instruments. These are forbidden, and indeed the difference between them and a war drum is clear.

Source: J. O'Kinealy, "Translation of an Arabic Pamphlet on the History and Doctrines of the Wahhabis," *Journal of the Asiatic Society of Bengal* 43 (1874): 68–82.

Source 15.6
The Poetry of Kabir

Early modern India was a place of much religious creativity and the interaction of various traditions. The majority of India's people practiced one or another of the many forms of Hinduism, while its Mughal rulers and perhaps 20 percent of the population were Muslims. And a new religion — Sikhism — took shape in the sixteenth century as well. Certainly there was tension and sometimes conflict among these religious communities, but not all was hostility across religious boundaries. In the writings of Kabir (1440–1518), perhaps India's most beloved poet, the sectarian differences among these religions dissolved into a mystical and transcendent love of the Divine in all of its many forms. Born into a family of Muslim weavers, Kabir as a young man became a student of a famous Hindu ascetic, Ramananda. Kabir's own poetry was and remains revered among Hindus, Muslims, and Sikhs alike. Source 15.6 contains selections from his poetry, translated by the famous Indian writer Rabindranath Tagore in the early twentieth century.

Questions to consider as you examine the source:

- In what ways was Kabir critical of conventional religious practice — both Muslim and Hindu?

- How would you describe Kabir's religious vision?

- How might more orthodox Hindus and Muslims respond to Kabir? How would the Wahhabis in particular take issue with Kabir's religious outlook?

KABIR

Poetry

ca. Late Fifteenth Century

O servant, where dost thou seek Me? Lo! I am beside thee.
I am neither in temple nor in mosque: I am neither in Kaaba [central shrine of Islam] nor in Kailash [a mountain sacred to Hindus]
Neither am I in rites and ceremonies, nor in Yoga and renunciation.
If thou art a true seeker, thou shalt at once see Me: . . . Kabir says, "O Sadhu! [a Hindu ascetic seeker] God is the breath of all breath."

It is needless to ask of a saint the caste to which he belongs;
For the priest, the warrior, the tradesman, and all the thirty-six castes, alike are seeking for God. The barber has sought God, the washerwoman, and the carpenter —
Even Raidas [a low-caste poet] was a seeker after God.
The Rishi Swapacha was a tanner by caste [an untouchable].
Hindus and Moslems alike have achieved that End, where remains no mark of distinction.

Within this earthen vessel [the human body] are bowers and groves, and within it is the Creator:
Within this vessel are the seven oceans and the unnumbered stars.
The touchstone and the jewel-appraiser are within;

And within this vessel the Eternal soundeth, and the spring wells up.
Kabir says: "Listen to me, my Friend! My beloved Lord is within."

Your Lord is near: yet you are climbing the palm-tree to seek Him.
The Brâhman priest goes from house to house and initiates people into faith:
Alas! the true fountain of life is beside you, and you have set up a stone to worship.
Kabir says: "I may never express how sweet my Lord is.
Yoga and the telling of beads, virtue and vice — these are naught to Him."

I do not ring the temple bell:
I do not set the idol on its throne:
I do not worship the image with flowers.
It is not the austerities that mortify the flesh which are pleasing to the Lord,
When you leave off your clothes and kill your senses, you do not please the Lord.
The man who is kind and who practices righteousness, who remains passive amidst the affairs of the world, who considers all creatures on earth as his own self,
He attains the Immortal Being, the true God is ever with him.

There is nothing but water at the holy bathing places;
And I know that they are useless, for I have bathed in
* them.*
The images are all lifeless, they cannot speak; I know,
* for I have cried aloud to them.*
The Purana [Hindu religious texts] and the Koran
* [Quran] are mere words; lifting up the curtain, I*
* have seen.*

Kabir gives utterance to the words of experience;
* and he knows very well that all other things are*
* untrue.*

Source: Rabindranath Tagore, trans., *The Songs of Kabir* (New York: Macmillan, 1915).

Source 15.7
Religious Syncretism in Indian Art

Another site of religious blending in early modern India took shape at the court of the Mughal emperor. Akbar presided over what we might now call interfaith gatherings and created a blended religious cult for Mughal elites. European-style religious art, painted by Mughal artists, appeared prominently at court, featuring scenes including Jesus, Mary, and various Christian saints.

The Muslim rulers of the Mughal Empire were also taking a growing interest in that ancient Hindu mind-body practice known as yoga. Some of the sultans seemed persuaded that such postures and practices conveyed great power that might well benefit themselves. Around 1550, a Muslim Sufi master closely connected to the Mughal court, Muhammad Gwaliyari, compiled systematic descriptions of twenty-two yoga postures, hoping to incorporate them into Sufi spiritual practice. Somewhat later, the Muslim prince Salim, who subsequently became the emperor Jahangir, commissioned a Hindu artist to illustrate this text, known as *The Ocean of Life*. In some of these illustrations, such as the one reproduced here, the yogi's face is painted to resemble that of Jesus, as depicted in the European religious literature then circulating in the Mughal court. Such images represented a remarkable cultural blending of Islamic patrons, Hindu practice, and Christian traditions.

Questions to consider as you examine the source:

■ Why might Muslim rulers and Sufi masters want to incorporate Hindu-based yoga techniques into their own practices?

■ What does the painting of a yogi with the face of Christ suggest about Indian views of Jesus?

■ What do such paintings imply about relationships across religious lines in early modern India? How might Kabir respond to this painting?

Kumbhaka (breathing exercises)

Renewal and Reform in the Early Modern World

1. **Comparing views of human potential:** What different understandings of human potential might you infer from these sources? What do those who created them believe is necessary to realize or fulfill that potential?

2. **Comparing religious reformers:** Consider the religious outlooks of Luther, al-Wahhab, and Kabir. What similarities and differences can you identify?

3. **Imagining a conversation:** Construct an imaginary debate or conversation between Condorcet and one or more of the religious or spiritually inclined authors of these sources.

Note

1. Robert S. Miola, ed., *Early Modern Catholicism: An Anthology of Primary Sources* (Oxford: Oxford University Press, 2007), 59.

CHAPTER 16

THINKING THROUGH SOURCES

Claiming Rights

In the discourse of the age of Atlantic revolutions, no idea had a more enduring resonance than that of "rights" — natural rights, political and civic rights, and "the rights of man" or, in a more recent expression, "human rights." However these rights were defined, they were understood as both natural and universal. They were considered inherent in the human condition rather than granted by some authority, and they were envisioned as being the same for everyone rather than depending on a person's birth, rank, or status in society. Growing out of the European Enlightenment, this understanding of "rights" was genuinely revolutionary, challenging almost all notions of government and society prior to the late eighteenth century. But even among supporters, the idea of human rights was highly controversial. What precisely were these rights? Did they support or contradict one another? Did they really apply equally to women and slaves? How should they be established and maintained? Such questions were central to this age of revolution and have informed much of the world's political history ever since.

Source 16.1
The French Revolution and the "Rights of Man"

The most prominent example of the language of rights found expression during the French Revolution in the Declaration of the Rights of Man and Citizen. It was a document hammered out in the French National Assembly early in that revolutionary upheaval and adopted at the end of August 1789. It has long been viewed as the philosophical core of the French Revolution.

Clearly the French document bore similarities to the language of the U.S. Declaration of Independence, for both drew on the ideas of the European Enlightenment. Furthermore, Thomas Jefferson, who largely wrote the U.S. Declaration, served as the ambassador to France at this time and was in close contact with Marquis de Lafayette, the principal author of the French Declaration. And Lafayette in turn had earlier served with the American revolutionary forces seeking independence from England.

Questions to consider as you examine the source:

- What purposes did the writers of the Declaration expect it to fulfill?

- What specific rights are spelled out in this document? What rights does it omit?

- What was revolutionary about the Declaration? What grievances against the old regime did the Declaration reflect?

The Declaration of the Rights of Man and Citizen
1789

The representatives of the French people, constituted as a National Assembly, and considering that ignorance, neglect, or contempt of the rights of man are the sole causes of public misfortunes and governmental corruption, have resolved to set forth in a solemn declaration the natural, inalienable and sacred rights of man. . . .

1. Men are born and remain free and equal in rights. Social distinctions may be based only on common utility.

2. The purpose of all political association is the preservation of the natural and imprescriptible rights of man. These rights are liberty, property, security, and resistance to oppression.

3. The principle of all sovereignty rests essentially in the nation. No body and no individual may exercise authority which does not emanate expressly from the nation.

4. Liberty consists in the ability to do whatever does not harm another; hence the exercise of the natural rights of each man has no other limits than those which assure to other members of society the enjoyment of the same rights. These limits can only be determined by the law.

5. The law only has the right to prohibit those actions which are injurious to society. No hindrance should be put in the way of anything not prohibited by the law, nor may any one be forced to do what the law does not require.

6. The law is the expression of the general will. All citizens have the right to take part, in person or by their representatives, in its formation. It must be the same for everyone whether it protects or penalizes. All citizens being equal in its eyes are equally admissible to all public dignities, offices, and employments, according to their ability, and with no other distinction than that of their virtues and talents.

7. No man may be indicted, arrested, or detained except in cases determined by the law and according to the forms which it has prescribed. . . .

9. Every man being presumed innocent until judged guilty, if it is deemed indispensable to arrest him, all rigor unnecessary to securing his person should be severely repressed by the law.

10. No one should be disturbed for his opinions, even in religion, provided that their manifestation does not trouble public order as established by law.

11. The free communication of thoughts and opinions is one of the most precious of the rights of man. Every citizen may therefore speak, write, and print freely, if he accepts his own responsibility for any abuse of this liberty in the cases set by the law.

12. The safeguard of the rights of man and the citizen requires public powers. These powers are therefore instituted for the advantage of all, and not for the private benefit of those to whom they are entrusted.

13. For maintenance of public authority and for expenses of administration, common taxation is indispensable. It should be apportioned equally among all the citizens according to their capacity to pay. . . .

17. Property being an inviolable and sacred right, no one may be deprived of it except when public necessity, certified by law, obviously requires it, and on the condition of a just compensation in advance.

Source: From *The French Revolution and Human Rights: A Brief Documentary History*. Edited, translated, and with an Introduction by Lynn Hunt. Copyright © 1996 by Bedford/St. Martin's. Used by permission of the publisher.

Source 16.2
Representing the Declaration

In the months that followed the drafting of the Declaration of the Rights of Man and Citizen, the new authorities worked to spread the Declaration's revolutionary ideas among the population. Perhaps the most iconic representation of the Declaration to appear in the months following its promulgation was a painting created by Jean-Jacques Le Barbier (1738–1826). Like many other artists who have sought to publicize and assert the legitimacy of radically new ideas, he drew heavily on older, established symbols and artistic conventions to convey his message. Thus, Le Barbier reproduced the text of the Declaration on tablets similar to those used in religious paintings to represent the Ten Commandments brought down by Moses from Mount Sinai. The two easily identifiable symbolic female figures — the winged allegorical figure representing Fame and the other personifying France — conveyed the virtue of and the audience for the Declaration's articles. Throughout the painting, Le Barbier used common classical symbols to provide visual cues to help his audience interpret its message, like the snake biting its tail representing eternity, the broken chains in the hands of France representing victory over oppression, and the laurel wreath of glory draped over the tablets. One symbol in particular, the red bonnet or "Phrygian," would have resonated with Le Barbier's audience. It was of ancient Greek origin but had become a popular symbol of the new French nation. Engravings of Le Barbier's painting were printed in large numbers and circulated across the kingdom, spreading the Declaration's ideas and Le Barbier's visual tribute to them to a broad audience.

Questions to consider as you examine the source:

- Why do you think that Le Barbier used well-known figures, symbols, and imagery in his painting? Why did the artist adorn the image with only female figures?

- What message is conveyed by placing the Declaration of the Rights of Man and Citizen on tablets evoking the Ten Commandments?

- The whole composition is overseen by the eye of God the Creator radiating from a triangle that by the late eighteenth century had both biblical and Masonic connotations. What does this symbol add to the composition?

Declaration of the Rights of Man and Citizen (Painting)

Source 16.3
Rights and National Independence

If the "rights of man" could be mobilized on behalf of individuals against an oppressive class system as in France, those rights came to be applied also to oppressed peoples, nations, and colonial subjects, as in the United States, Haiti, and Latin America and later all across Asia and Africa. In a well-known letter, written in 1815, Simón Bolívar, a prominent political and military leader in the struggle against Spanish rule in Latin America, made the case for the independence of his continent, arguing that Latin Americans' collective "rights," derived from Europe itself, had been massively violated.

Questions to consider as you examine the source:

■ What understanding of "rights" informed Bolívar's demand for independence? Why did he feel that the situation of his people was so "extraordinary and complicated"?

■ What were his chief objections to Spanish rule?

■ What difficulties did Bolívar foresee in achieving the kind of stable and unified independence that he so much desired?

SIMÓN BOLÍVAR
The Jamaica Letter
1815

Success will crown our efforts, because the destiny of [Latin] America has been irrevocably decided; the tie that bound her to Spain has been severed. . . . The hatred that the Peninsula has inspired in us is greater than the ocean between us. It would be easier to have the two continents meet than to reconcile the spirits of the two countries. The habit of obedience; a community of interest, of understanding, of religion; mutual goodwill; a tender regard for the birthplace and good name of our forefathers; in short, all that gave rise to our hopes, came to us from Spain. . . . At present the contrary attitude persists: we are threatened with the fear of death, dishonor, and every harm; there is nothing we have not suffered at the hands of that unnatural stepmother — Spain. The veil has been torn asunder. . . . For this reason America fights desperately. . . .

We are, moreover, neither Indian nor European, but a species midway between the legitimate proprietors of this country and the Spanish usurpers. In short, though Americans by birth we derive our rights from Europe, and we have to assert these rights against the rights of the natives, and at the same time we must defend ourselves against the invaders. This places us in a most extraordinary and involved situation. . . .

The role of the inhabitants of the American hemisphere has for centuries been purely passive. Politically they were nonexistent. We are still in a position lower than slavery, and therefore it is more difficult for us to rise to the enjoyment of freedom. . . . We have been harassed by a conduct which has not only deprived us of our rights but has kept us in a sort of permanent infancy with regard to public affairs.

Americans today . . . occupy a position in society no better than that of serfs destined for labor, or at best they have no more status than that of mere consumers. Yet even this status is surrounded with galling restrictions, such as being forbidden to grow European crops, or to store products which are royal monopolies, or to establish factories of a type the Peninsula itself does not possess. To this add the exclusive trading privileges, even in articles of prime necessity, and the barriers between American provinces, designed to prevent all exchange of trade, traffic, and understanding. In short, do you wish to know what our future held? — simply the cultivation of the fields of indigo, grain, coffee, sugar cane, cacao, and cotton; cattle raising on the broad plains; hunting wild game in the jungles; digging in the earth to mine its gold — but even these limitations could never satisfy the greed of Spain. . . . Is it not an outrage and a violation of human rights to expect a land so splendidly endowed, so vast, rich, and populous, to remain merely passive? . . .

We were cut off and, as it were, removed from the world in relation to the science of government and administration of the state. We were never viceroys or governors, save in the rarest of instances; seldom archbishops and bishops; diplomats never; as military men, only subordinates; as nobles, without royal privileges. In brief, we were neither magistrates nor financiers and seldom merchants. . . .

These laws favor, almost exclusively, the natives of the country who are of Spanish extraction. Thus . . . those born in America have been despoiled of their constitutional rights. . . .

The American provinces are fighting for their freedom, and they will ultimately succeed. . . . It is a grandiose idea to think of consolidating the New World into a single nation, united by pacts into a single bond. It is reasoned that, as these parts have a common origin, language, customs, and religion, they ought to have a single government to permit the newly formed states to unite in a confederation. But this is not possible. Actually, America is separated by climatic differences, geographic diversity, conflicting interests, and dissimilar characteristics. . . . This type of organization may come to pass in some happier period of our regeneration. . . .

As soon as we are strong and under the guidance of a liberal nation which will lend us her protection, we will achieve accord in cultivating the virtues and talents that lead to glory. Then will we march majestically toward that great prosperity for which South America is destined. Then will those sciences and arts which, born in the East, have enlightened Europe, wing their way to a free Colombia, which will cordially bid them welcome.

Source: Francisco Javier Yanes y Cristóbal Mendoza Montilla: Colección de documentos relativos a la vida pública del Libertador de Colombia y del Perú Simón Bolívar para servir a la historia de la independencia de Suramérica, Caracas, 1833, T. XXII, pp. 207–29. Translated by Suzanne Sturn. Used by permission of Suzanne Sturn.

Source 16.4
Rights and Slavery: "Reason and Nature"

The language of "rights," derived from the French Revolution, had implications for race relations and the long-established practice of slavery, as well as for colonial rule. France legally abolished slavery in its colonies in 1794, though it was restored by Napoleon in 1802. The contradiction between the "rights of man," racial inequality, and, by implication, slavery was addressed in an engraving produced in 1793, the year before slavery was abolished, titled "All Mortals Are Equal, It Is Not Birth but Virtue That Makes the

Difference." The allegorical figure at the center of the image is Reason, with the sacred flame of "love of the fatherland" emerging from her head. She places a level on a white man and a man of color, behind whom is a cornucopia of abundance. The man of color holds in one hand the Declaration of the Rights of Man and Citizen (1789) and in the other the Decree of May 15, 1791, which granted free blacks and mulattoes political rights. Reason is pushed by the allegorical figure of Nature, who is seated on a sack out of which flee the demons labeled Aristocracy, Selfishness, Injustice, and Insurrection. While this image celebrates political rights granted to free blacks and mulattoes, it could also be read as advocating the same rights for slaves at a time when France was edging toward emancipation legislation.

Questions to consider as you examine the source:

■ What role do the allegorical figures of Reason and Nature play in this scene?

■ What does the level symbolize in this image? What meaning might you derive from the fact that the man of color is depicted in a loincloth, while the white man is fully clothed?

■ How might a supporter of slave emancipation interpret this scene? How might an opponent?

All Mortals Are Equal, It Is Not Birth but Virtue That Makes the Difference

Source 16.5
Rights and Slavery:
An African American Voice

In the United States, the language of the Declaration of Independence, with its affirmation that "all men are created equal," stood in glaring contrast to the brutal realities of slavery. In a famous speech, Frederick Douglass forcefully highlighted that great contradiction in the new American nation. Born a slave in 1818, Douglass had escaped from bondage to become a leading abolitionist, writer, newspaper publisher, and African American spokesperson. He was invited to address an antislavery meeting in Rochester, New York, on July 4, 1852.

Questions to consider as you examine the source:

■ On what basis does Douglass demand the end of slavery? How do his arguments relate to the ideology of the American Revolution?

■ How would you describe the rhetorical strategy of his speech?

■ Why, in the end, can Douglass claim, "I do not despair of this country"? What are the "forces in operation, which must inevitably work the downfall of slavery"?

FREDERICK DOUGLASS

What to the Slave Is the Fourth of July?
1852

Fellow-citizens, pardon me, allow me to ask, why am I called upon to speak here to-day? What have I, or those I represent, to do with your national independence? Are the great principles of political freedom and of natural justice, embodied in that Declaration of Independence, extended to us? and am I, therefore, called upon to bring our humble offering to the national altar, and to confess the benefits and express devout gratitude for the blessings resulting from your independence to us?

Would to God, both for your sakes and ours, that an affirmative answer could be truthfully returned to these questions! . . .

But, such is not the state of the case. I say it with a sad sense of the disparity between us. I am not included within the pale of this glorious anniversary! Your high independence only reveals the immeasurable distance between us. . . . This Fourth [of] July is yours, not mine. . . . You may rejoice, I must mourn.

I shall see, this day . . . from the slave's point of view. . . . I do not hesitate to declare, with all my soul, that the character and conduct of this nation never looked blacker to me than on this 4th of July! . . . Standing with God and the crushed and bleeding slave on this occasion, I will . . . dare to call in question and to denounce, with all the emphasis I can command, everything that serves to perpetuate slavery — the great sin and shame of America!

For the present, it is enough to affirm the equal manhood of the Negro race. Is it not astonishing that . . . while we are engaged in all manner of enterprises common to other men . . . , we are called upon to prove that we are men!

Would you have me argue that man is entitled to liberty? that he is the rightful owner of his own body? You have already declared it. Must I argue the wrongfulness of slavery? Is that a question for Republicans? . . .

At a time like this, scorching irony, not convincing argument, is needed. . . . For it is not light that is needed, but fire. . . . [T]he conscience of the nation must be roused; . . . the hypocrisy of the nation must be exposed; and its crimes against God and man must be proclaimed and denounced.

What, to the American slave, is your 4th of July? I answer: a day that reveals to him, more than all other days in the year, the gross injustice and cruelty to which he is the constant victim. To him, your celebration is a sham; your boasted liberty, an unholy license; your national greatness, swelling vanity; your sounds of rejoicing are empty and heartless; your denunciations of tyrants, brass-fronted impudence; your shouts of liberty and equality, hollow mockery; your prayers and hymns, your sermons and thanksgivings, with all your religious parade, and solemnity, are, to him, mere bombast, fraud, deception, impiety, and hypocrisy — a thin veil to cover up crimes which would disgrace a nation of savages. There is not a nation on the earth guilty of practices, more shocking and bloody, than are the people of these United States, at this very hour. . . .

Fellow-citizens! I will not enlarge further on your national inconsistencies. The existence of slavery in this country brands your republicanism as a sham, your humanity as a base pretence, and your Christianity as a lie. It destroys your moral power abroad; it corrupts your politicians at home. It saps the foundation of religion; it makes your name a hissing, and a byword to a mocking earth. It is the antagonistic force in your government, the only thing that seriously disturbs and endangers your Union. It fetters your progress; it is the enemy of improvement, the deadly foe of education; it fosters pride; it breeds insolence; it promotes vice; it shelters crime; it is a curse to the earth that supports it; and yet, you cling to it, as if it were the sheet anchor of all your hopes. Oh! be warned! be warned! a horrible reptile is coiled up in your nation's bosom; the venomous creature is nursing at the tender breast of your youthful republic; for the love of God, tear away, and fling from you the hideous monster, and let the weight of twenty millions crush and destroy it forever! . . .

Allow me to say, in conclusion . . . , I do not despair of this country. There are forces in operation, which must inevitably work the downfall of slavery. . . . While drawing encouragement from the Declaration of Independence, the great principles it contains, and the genius of American Institutions, my spirit is also cheered by the obvious tendencies of the age. Nations do not now stand in the same relation to each other that they did ages ago. No nation can now shut itself up from the surrounding world, and trot round in the same old path of its fathers without interference. . . . But a change has now come over the affairs of mankind. Walled cities and empires have become unfashionable. The arm of commerce has borne away the gates of the strong city. Intelligence is penetrating the darkest corners of the globe. It makes its pathway over and under the sea, as well as on the earth. Wind, steam, and lightning are its chartered agents. Oceans no longer divide, but link nations together. From Boston to London is now a holiday excursion. Space is comparatively annihilated. Thoughts expressed on one side of the Atlantic are distinctly heard on the other. The far off and almost fabulous Pacific rolls in grandeur at our feet. The Celestial Empire, the mystery of ages, is being solved. The fiat of the Almighty, "Let there be Light," has not yet spent its force.

Source: Frederick Douglass, "What to the Slave Is the Fourth of July?," July 5, 1852, *Africans in America*, PBS Online, http://www .pbs.org/wgbh/aia/part4/4h2927t.html.

Source 16.6
The Rights of Women: "Frenchwomen Freed"

Did the "rights of man" include women? During the French Revolution, the question of women's rights was sharply debated. Just two years after the famous French Declaration, the French playwright and journalist Olympe de Gouges sought to apply those rights to women when she crafted her *Declaration of the Rights of Woman and the Female Citizen.* "Woman, wake up," she wrote, "the tocsin [warning bell] of reason is being heard throughout the whole universe; discover your rights."[1] As the revolution unfolded, many women became actively involved, taking part in street demonstrations, establishing dozens of women's clubs, and petitioning legislative bodies on behalf of women. Most men, however, even ardent revolutionaries, agreed with the French lawyer Jean-Denis Lanjuinais that "the physique of women, their goal in life [marriage and motherhood], and their position distance them from the exercise of a great number of political rights and duties."[2] In late 1793, all women's clubs were officially prohibited. But in the same year, the posture of these increasingly assertive women found expression in an anonymous engraving titled "Frenchwomen Freed." The woman's cap displays the tricolor cockade that came to symbolize the revolution; she carries a pike inscribed with the slogan "liberty or death"; the medal on her waistband reads: "Liberty, armed with a pike, is victorious, July 14 [Bastille Day]."

Questions to consider as you examine the source:

- How would you read the overall message of this engraving?

- How does her physical stance and facial expression contribute to this message?

- What might attract such women to the cause of the revolution?

French Woman during the Revolution

Source 16.7
The Rights of Women:
An American Feminist Voice

Throughout the nineteenth century, debates about the rights of women echoed loudly across Europe, North America, and beyond. Among the most well-known and eloquent appeals for these rights came from the American feminist leader Elizabeth Cady Stanton (1815–1902) in an 1892 address to a U.S. congressional committee. She was urging then, as she had for decades, an amendment to the Constitution giving women the right to vote. That effort was finally successful in 1920, almost two decades after Stanton died.

Questions to consider as you examine the source:

■ What kind of rights was Stanton seeking for women? Do you think she was advocating a reform of gender relations or a more revolutionary transformation?

■ How might you summarize in your own words her argument as to why women should have such rights?

■ How might women and men with other points of view have argued with Stanton?

ELIZABETH CADY STANTON
The Solitude of Self
1892

The point I wish plainly to bring before you on this occasion is the individuality of each human soul. . . . In discussing the rights of woman, we are to consider, first, what belongs to her as an individual, in a world of her own. . . .

The strongest reason for giving woman all the opportunities for higher education, for the full development of her faculties . . . ; for giving her the most enlarged freedom of thought and action; a complete emancipation from all forms of bondage, of custom, dependence, superstition; from all the crippling influences of fear, is the solitude and personal responsibility of her own individual life. The strongest reason why we ask for woman a voice in the government under which she lives; in the religion she is asked to believe; equality in social life, where she is the chief factor; a place in the trades and professions, where she may earn her bread, is because of her birthright to self-sovereignty; because, as an individual, she must rely on herself. No matter how much women prefer to lean, to be protected and supported, nor how much men desire to have them do so, they must make the voyage of life alone. . . . It matters not whether the solitary voyager is man or woman. . . . Alike amid the greatest triumphs and darkest tragedies of life we walk alone. . . .

In [old] age, when the pleasures of youth are passed, children grown up, married and gone, the hurry and hustle of life in a measure over, when the hands are weary of active service, when the old armchair and the fireside are the chosen resorts, then men and women alike must fall back on their own resources. . . .

If from a lifelong participation in public affairs a woman feels responsible for the laws regulating our system of education, the discipline of our jails and prisons, the sanitary conditions of our private homes, public buildings, and thoroughfares, an interest in commerce, finance, our foreign relations, in any or all of these questions, her solitude will at least be respectable. . . .

Seeing then that the responsibilities of life rests equally on man and woman, that their destiny is the same, they need the same preparation for time and eternity. The talk of sheltering woman from the fierce storms of life is the sheerest mockery, for they beat on her from every point of the compass, just as they do on man, and with more fatal results, for he has been trained to protect himself, to resist, to conquer. . . . Whatever the theories may be of woman's dependence on man, in the supreme moments of her life he cannot bear her burdens. . . .

[T]here is a solitude, which each and every one of us has always carried with him, more inaccessible than the ice-cold mountains, more profound than the midnight sea; the solitude of self. Our inner being, which we call ourself, no eye nor touch of man or angel has ever pierced. . . . Who, I ask you, can take, dare take, on himself the rights, the duties, the responsibilities of another human soul?

Source: Elizabeth Cady Stanton, "The Solitude of Self," address delivered before the Committee of the Judiciary of the United States Congress, January 18, 1892. The Library of Congress.

ESSAY QUESTIONS

Claiming Rights

1. **Considering ideas and circumstances:** Historians frequently debate the relative importance of ideas in shaping historical events. What impact do you think the ideas about rights expressed in these documents had on the historical development of the Atlantic world and beyond? And what specific historical contexts or conditions shaped the understanding of "rights" expressed in each of these sources?

2. **Making comparisons:** Which sources speak more about individual rights, and which focus attention on collective rights? What common understandings can you identify?

3. **Imagining a conversation:** How might the creators of these sources have responded to one another? What points of agreement might they share? What differences might arise in a conversation among them?

4. **Defining a common origin:** In what respects did each of these sources derive from the French Revolution?

Notes

1. Olympe de Gouges, "The Rights of Women," in *The French Revolution and Human Rights: A Brief Documentary History*, edited and translated by Lynn Hunt (Boston: Bedford/St. Martin's, 1996), 124–29.

2. Jean-Denis Lanjuinais, "Discussion of Citizenship under the Proposed New Constitution," in Hunt, *The French Revolution and Human Rights*, 133.

CHAPTER 17

Experiencing the Early Industrial Revolution

The immense economic and social changes of the Industrial Revolution left almost no one untouched in the societies that experienced it most fully. Especially in its early phases (roughly 1780–1875), that immense transformation generated a traumatic upheaval in ways of living for many people. For others, it brought new opportunities, wealth, and comfort. In seeking to understand how individuals experienced this unprecedented revolutionary process, historians have at their disposal a wealth of evidence, both documentary and visual. Each of the sources that follow provides just a glimpse of what living through those early decades of the Industrial Revolution may have meant to those who experienced it, mostly in England where it all began.

Source 17.1
The Experience of an English Factory Worker

The early Industrial Revolution represented not only a technological breakthrough of epic proportions but also a transformation in the organization of work, expressed most fully in the factory. Unlike the artisan's workshop, which it largely replaced, the factory concentrated human labor in a single place and separated workers from the final product by assigning them highly specialized and repetitive tasks. In the name of efficiency and productivity, owners and managers imposed strict discipline in their factories and regulated workers' lives according to clock time. Finally, workers were wage earners, dependent for their economic survival on a very modest income and highly uncertain employment, both of which were subject to the vagaries of the market. One such worker was Elizabeth Bentley, who had worked in a factory since the age of six. In 1831, when she was twenty-three years old, Bentley testified before a British parliamentary committee investigating conditions in textile mills. A subsequent inquiry elicited testimony from William Harter, a mill owner. As a result of these investigations, legislation in 1833 limited the hours of employment for women and children.

Questions to consider as you examine the sources:

■ Child labor was nothing new, for children had long worked in the fields and workshops of preindustrial Europe. What was different about the conditions under which children worked in early industrial factories?

■ Why do you think the investigator queried Elizabeth Bentley specifically about the treatment of girls?

■ How does William Harter's testimony explain the willingness of factory owners to impose these conditions on their workers? How might he respond to Elizabeth Bentley's testimony?

Source 17.1A
ELIZABETH BENTLEY, FACTORY WORKER

Testimony
1831

What age are you? — Twenty-three.

Where do you live? — At Leeds.

What time did you begin to work at a factory? — When I was six years old.

What kind of mill is it? — Flax-mill.

What was your business in that mill? — I was a little doffer [cleaner of the machines].

What were your hours of labour in that mill? — From 5 in the morning till 9 at night, when they were thronged [busy].

For how long a time together have you worked that excessive length of time? — For about half a year.

What were your usual hours when you were not so thronged? — From 6 in the morning till 7 at night.

What time was allowed for your meals? — Forty minutes at noon.

Had you any time to get your breakfast or drinking? — No, we got it as we could.

Explain what it is you had to do? — When the frames are full, they have to stop the frames, and take the flyers off, and take the full bobbins off, and carry them to the roller; and then put empty ones on, and set the frame going again.

Does that keep you constantly on your feet? — Yes, there are so many frames, and they run so quick.

Suppose you flagged a little, or were too late, what would they do? — Strap us.

Are they in the habit of strapping those who are last in doffing? — Yes.

Constantly? — Yes.

Girls as well as boys? — Yes.

Have you ever been strapped? — Yes.

Severely? — Yes.

Were the girls struck so as to leave marks upon their skin? — Yes, they have had black marks many times, and their parents dare not come to him about it, they were afraid of losing their work.

Could you eat your food well in that factory? — No, indeed I had not much to eat, and the little I had I could not eat it, my appetite was so poor, and being covered with dust; and it was no use to take it home, I could not eat it, and the overlooker took it, and gave it to the pigs.

How far had you to go for dinner? — We could not go home to dinner.

Where did you dine? — In the mill.

Did you live far from the mill? — Yes, two miles.

Supposing you had not been in time enough in the morning at these mills, what would have been the consequence? — We should have been quartered. If we were a quarter of an hour too late, they would take off half an hour; we only got a penny an hour, and they would take a half-penny more.

Were you also beaten for being too late? — No, I was never beaten myself, I have seen the boys beaten for being too late.

Were you generally there in time? — Yes; my mother had been up at 4 o'clock in the morning, and at 2 o'clock in the morning; the colliers used to go to their work about 3 or 4 o'clock, and when she heard them stirring she has got up out of her warm bed, and gone out and asked them the time; and I have sometimes been at Hunslet Car at 2 o'clock in the morning, when it was streaming down with rain, and we have had to stay until the mill was opened.

Source 17.1B
WILLIAM HARTER, MILL OWNER
Testimony
1832

What effect would it have on your manufacture to reduce the hours of labor to ten?— It would instantly much reduce the value of my mill and machinery, and consequently far prejudice my manufacture. . . . To produce the same quantity of work under a ten-hours bill will require an additional outlay of 3,000 or 4,000 pounds; therefore a ten-hours bill would impose upon me the necessity of this additional outlay in such perishable property as buildings and machinery, or I must be content to relinquish one-sixth portion of my business.

Source: *British Sessional Papers*, vol. 15 (London, 1832), 195196; vol. 21, pt. D-3 (London, 1833), 2628.

Source 17.2
Urban Living Conditions

If factory working conditions were deplorable in the early decades of the English Industrial Revolution, the urban living conditions for many of those workers were no less horrific. In a classic description of industrial Manchester in the early 1840s, a twenty-four-year-old Friedrich Engels, later a close collaborator with Karl Marx, provided a vivid portrait of urban working-class life in England's premier industrial city. By the time his German-language account was translated into English in 1886, Engels acknowledged that "the most crying abuses described in this book have either disappeared or have been made less conspicuous." He added, however, that broadly similar conditions were prevalent in later-industrializing countries such as France, Germany, and the United States.

Questions to consider as you examine the source:

- How does Engels describe working-class life in Manchester in the early 1840s?

- What implied contrasts does Engels make with the earlier rural life of poor peasants?

- To what does he attribute these conditions?

FRIEDRICH ENGELS

The Condition of the Working Class in England
1844

Manchester contains about four hundred thousand inhabitants. . . . The town itself is peculiarly built, so that a person may live in it for years, and go in and out daily without coming into contact with a working-people's quarter or even with workers, that is, so long as he confines himself to his business or to pleasure walks. This arises chiefly from the fact, that by unconscious tacit agreement, as well as with outspoken conscious determination, the working people's quarters are sharply separated from the sections of the city reserved for the middle-class. . . .

Here [in Old Town Manchester] one is in an almost undisguised working-men's quarter, for even the shops and beer houses hardly take the trouble to exhibit a trifling degree of cleanliness. But all this is nothing in comparison with the courts and lanes which lie behind, to which access can be gained only through covered passages, in which no two human beings can pass at the same time. Of the irregular cramming together of dwellings in ways which defy all rational plan, of the tangle in which they are crowded literally one upon the other, it is impossible to convey an idea. Right and left a multitude of covered passages lead from the main street into numerous courts, and he who turns in thither gets into a filth and disgusting grime, the equal of which is not to be found. . . .

In one of these courts there stands directly at the entrance, at the end of the covered passage, a privy without a door, so dirty that the inhabitants can pass into and out of the court only by passing through foul pools of stagnant urine and excrement. . . . Below it on the river there are several tanneries which fill the whole neighbourhood with the stench of animal putrefaction. Below Ducie Bridge the only entrance to most of the houses is by means of narrow, dirty stairs and over heaps of refuse and filth. The first court below Ducie Bridge, known as Allen's Court, was in such a state at the time of the cholera that the sanitary police ordered it evacuated, swept, and disinfected with chloride of lime. . . . At the bottom flows, or rather stagnates, the Irk [River], a narrow, coal-black, foul-smelling stream, full of debris and refuse. . . .

In dry weather, a long string of the most disgusting, blackish-green, slime pools are left standing on this bank, from the depths of which bubbles of miasmatic gas constantly arise and give forth a stench. . . . Above the bridge are tanneries, bone mills, and gasworks, from which all drains and refuse find their way into the Irk, which receives further the contents of all the neighbouring sewers and privies. It may be easily imagined, therefore, what sort of residue the stream deposits. Here the background embraces the pauper burial-ground, the station of the Liverpool and Leeds railway, and, in the rear of this, the Workhouse [where the desperately poor found shelter and employment], . . .

which, like a citadel, looks threateningly down from behind its high walls and parapets on the hilltop, upon the working-people's quarter below.

Passing along a rough bank, among stakes and washing-lines, one penetrates into this chaos of small one-storied, one-roomed huts, in most of which there is no artificial floor; kitchen, living and sleeping-room all in one. In such a hole, scarcely five feet long by six broad, I found two beds — and such bedsteads and beds! — which, with a staircase and chimney-place, exactly filled the room. In several others I found absolutely nothing, while the door stood open, and the inhabitants leaned against it. Everywhere before the doors refuse and offal; that any sort of pavement lay underneath could not be seen but only felt, here and there, with the feet. This whole collection of cattle-sheds for human beings was surrounded on two sides by houses and a factory, and on the third by the river. . . .

In almost every court one or even several such pens [of pigs] may be found, into which the inhabitants of the court throw all refuse and offal, whence the swine grow fat; and the atmosphere, confined on all four sides, is utterly corrupted by putrefying animal and vegetable substances. . . .

Such is the Old Town of Manchester. . . . Everything which here arouses horror and indignation is of recent origin, belongs to the *industrial epoch.*

Source: Friedrich Engels, *The Condition of the Working Class in England in 1844* (London: Swan Sonnenschein & Co., 1892), 45, 48–53.

Source 17.3
Another View of Factory Life

As Engels admitted, early working and living conditions in industrial England had improved by the later nineteenth century, though the debate about factory life had hardly ended. Source 17.3, an 1874 painting by English artist Eyre Crowe, provides a more benevolent view of an industrial factory as it portrays a number of young women workers during their dinner hour outside the cotton textile mill in the industrial town of Wigan.

Questions to consider as you examine the source:

■ How does this depiction of factory life compare with that of Source 17.1? How might you account for the differences?

■ How do you respond to Crowe's painting? Do you think it was an honest portrayal of factory life for women? What might be missing?

■ Notice the details of the painting — the young women's relationship to one another, the hairnets on their heads, their clothing, their activities during this break from work. What marks them as working-class women? What impression of factory life did Crowe seek to convey? Was he trying to highlight or minimize the class differences of industrial Britain?

Outside the Factory

Manchester Art Gallery, UK/Bridgeman Images

Source 17.4
A Weaver's Lament

As industrialization generated new work in the factories, it also destroyed older means of livelihood, particularly that of skilled artisans. By the early 1860s, the silk weavers of Coventry, England, a long-established and previously thriving group of artisans, were in desperate straits, owing in part to a decline in the fashion of wearing silk ribbons. Many individual weavers had to sell their looms to the larger manufacturers who were organizing more efficient production in factories. The song that follows was sung by unemployed weavers as they paraded through the streets of Coventry on their way to relief work, often in stone quarries. It reflects the costs of the Industrial Revolution for a body of proud and skilled artisans and their distress at an economic system that seemed to cast them adrift.

Questions to consider as you examine the source:

■ Who or what does the song blame for the plight of the weavers?

■ What does the song mean by mentioning the "commercial plan" and "political economy"? And how do you understand the line "He's only a weaver that no one owns"?

■ How might you compare the life of an unemployed weaver with that of a factory worker like Elizabeth Bentley?

Only a Weaver
1860s

Who is that man coming up the street
With weary manner and shuffling feet;
With a face that tells of care and grief
And in hope that seems to have lost belief.
For wickedness past he now atones
He's only a weaver that no one owns.
He's coming no doubt from breaking stones
With saddened heart and aching bones.
But why should he grumble, he gets good pay
A loaf and six pence every day.
He thought if he worked both night and day
He ought to receive equivalent pay;
But he's just an inconsistent man
Who doesn't understand the commercial plan.
Political economy now must sway
And say when a man shall work or play.

If he's wanted his wages may be high
If he isn't, why then, he may starve and die.
If you employ him, don't mend the price
He's starving, you know and has no choice —
And give him to weave the worst of silk
For it's only a weaver's time you bilk. . . .
Yet take no heed of his sighs and groans
His careworn face, his agonized moans;
For wickedness past he now atones
He's only a weaver that no one owns.

Source: Joseph Gutteridge, *Light and Shadows in the Life of an Artisan* (1893), 153, abridged and adapted in *Poverty Knock*, edited by Roy Palmer (New York: Cambridge University Press, 1974), 24. Copyright © Cambridge University Press, 1974. Reprinted with permission of Cambridge University Press.

Source 17.5
Protest and Song

The travails of working-class life in the early industrial era stimulated protests of many kinds: the machine breaking of the Luddites; the strikes of trade unionists; and, increasingly prominent as the nineteenth century wore on, the organizational and political efforts of socialists. In 1871, a French working-class activist, poet, and songwriter named Eugène Pottier composed "The Internationale," a song that became the unofficial anthem of working-class and socialist movements. Source 17.5 offers an English translation made in 1900 by Charles Kerr, an American publisher of radical books. The song gave expression to both the oppression and the hopes of ordinary people as they worked for a socialist future.

Questions to consider as you examine the source:

■ What evidence of class consciousness is apparent in the song? What particular grievances are expressed in it?

■ How does "The Internationale" portray the struggle and the future?

■ What evidence of Marxist thinking can you find in its lyrics?

EUGÈNE POTTIER (TRANSLATED BY CHARLES KERR)

The Internationale

1871

Arise, ye prisoners of starvation!
Arise, ye wretched of the earth!
For justice thunders condemnation,
A better world's in birth!
No more tradition's chains shall bind us,
Arise ye slaves, no more in thrall!
The earth shall rise on new foundations,
We have been nought, we shall be all.

(Chorus:)
'Tis the final conflict,
Let each stand in his place.
The international working class
Shall be the human race.

We want no condescending saviors
To rule us from a judgment hall;
We workers ask not for their favors;
Let us consult for all.
To make the thief disgorge his booty
To free the spirit from its cell,
We must ourselves decide our duty,
We must decide, and do it well.
(Chorus)

The law oppresses us and tricks us,
wage slav'ry drains the workers' blood;
The rich are free from obligations,
The laws the poor delude.

Too long we've languished in subjection,
Equality has other laws;
"No rights," says she, "without their duties,
No claims on equals without cause."
(Chorus)

Behold them seated in their glory
The kings of mine and rail and soil!
What have you read in all their story,
But how they plundered toil?
Fruits of the workers' toil are buried
In the strong coffers of a few;
In working for their restitution
The men will only ask their due.
(Chorus)

Toilers from shops and fields united,
The union we of all who work;
The earth belongs to us, the workers,
No room here for the shirk.
How many on our flesh have fattened;
But if the noisome birds of prey
Shall vanish from the sky some morning,
The blessed sunlight still will stay.
(Chorus)

Source: Eugène Pottier, "The Internationale," translated by Charles Hope Kerr, in *Socialist Songs* (1900), Wikisource, http://en.wikisource.org/wiki/The_Internationale_(Kerr).

Source 17.6
Railroads and the Middle Class

Among the new experiences of the early industrial era for many people was railroad travel, made possible by the steam locomotive during the early nineteenth century. By 1850, Great Britain had almost 10,000 kilometers of railroad lines and Germany almost 6,000. To industrial age enthusiasts, it was a thing of wonder, power, and speed. Samuel Smiles, the nineteenth-century British advocate of self-help, thrift, and individualism, wrote rhapsodically of the railroad's beneficent effects:

> The iron rail proved a magicians' road. The locomotive gave a new celerity to time. It virtually reduced England to a sixth of its size. It brought the country nearer to the town and the town to the country. . . . It energized punctuality, discipline, and attention; and proved a moral teacher by the influence of example.[1]

Like almost everything else, railroads and railway travel were shaped by the social changes of the early industrial era, including the growth of a more numerous and prosperous middle class of industrialists, bankers, and educated professionals of various kinds. Such people invested heavily in railroads, spurring the rapid expansion of railways in Britain. Moreover, travel on the new trains was segregated by class. First-class passengers occupied luxurious compartments with upholstered seats; second-class travelers enjoyed rather less comfortable accommodations; and third-class travel, designed for the poor or working classes, originally took place in uncovered freight wagons, often with standing room only and located closest to the locomotive, where noise and the danger of fire were the greatest. In 1844, regulations required that third-class carriages be roofed.

Source 17.6, dating from the 1870s, illustrates this intersection of an emerging middle class and railway travel, showing a family in a railroad compartment, returning home from a vacation.

Questions to consider as you examine the source:

■ What attitude toward the railroad in particular and the industrial age in general does this image suggest?

■ What marks this family as middle class and their compartment as "first class"?

■ What does the poem at the top of the image suggest about the place of "home" in industrial Britain? How does the image itself present the railway car as a home away from home?

The Railroad as a Symbol of the Industrial Era

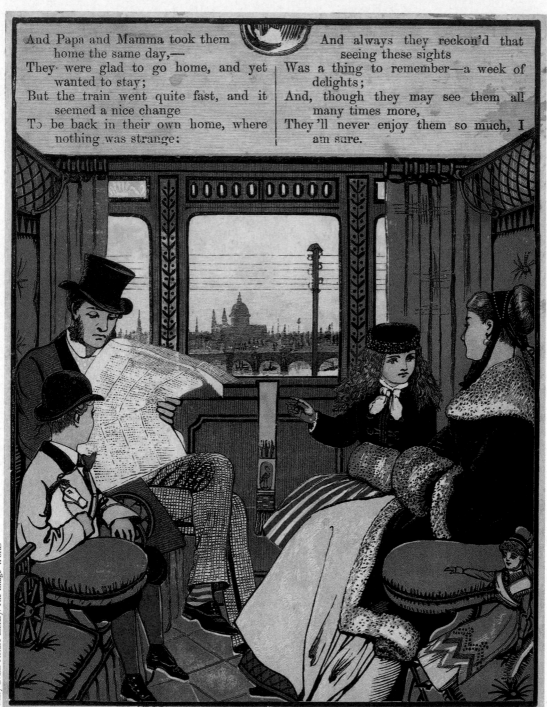

And Papa and Mamma took them
home the same day,—
They were glad to go home, and yet
wanted to stay;
But the train went quite fast, and it
seemed a nice change
To be back in their own home, where
nothing was strange:

And always they reckon'd that
seeing these sights
Was a thing to remember—a week of
delights;
And, though they may see them all
many times more,
They'll never enjoy them so much, I
am sure.

Source 17.7
Inequality

In the early industrial era, almost everyone became acutely aware of the sharp inequalities of social life. Of course, class differences had characterized all civilizations since ancient Egypt and Mesopotamia. But now those inequalities were experienced within the confined space of city life; they found expression in two relatively new social groups — the urban working class and the growing middle classes; and they occurred as democratic ideas and socialist movements challenged the ancient legitimacy of such inequalities. These features of the early industrial era are illustrated in Source 17.7, an image by British artist John Leech, published in 1843 in *Punch*, a magazine of humor and social satire.

Questions to consider as you examine the source:

■ How are the class differences of early industrial Britain represented in this image? Notice the depiction of the life of miners in the bottom panel.

■ How does this source connect the Industrial Revolution with Britain's colonial empire? Notice the figure in the upper right reclining in exotic splendor, perhaps in India.

■ To what extent does the image correspond to Friedrich Engels's description of industrial society in Source 17.2: Urban Living Conditions?

Capital and Labour

CAPITAL AND LABOUR.

Experiencing the Early Industrial Revolution

1. **Celebrating industrialization:** Based on these sources and the text of Chapter 17, construct an argument in celebration of the Industrial Revolution.

2. **Criticizing industrialization:** Construct an argument based on these sources and the text of Chapter 17 criticizing the Industrial Revolution.

3. **Considering images and written documents as evidence:** What are the strengths and limitations of visual sources, as compared to written documents, in helping historians understand the Industrial Revolution?

4. **Distinguishing capitalism and industrialization:** To what extent are these sources actually dealing with the Industrial Revolution itself, and in what ways are they addressing the economic system known as capitalism? How useful is this distinction for understanding the early industrial age?

Note

1. Quoted in Francis D. Klingender, *Art and the Industrial Revolution* (New York: Augustus M. Kelley, 1968), 139.

Colonial India: Experience and Response

India was Britain's "jewel in the crown," the centerpiece of its expanding empire in Asia and Africa. Until the late 1850s, Britain's growing involvement with South Asia was organized and led by the British East India Company, a private trading firm that had acquired a charter from the Crown allowing it to exercise military, political, and administrative functions in India as well as its own commercial operations. But after the explosive upheaval of the Indian Rebellion of 1857–1858, the British government itself assumed control of the region until India's independence in 1947.

Throughout the colonial era, the British relied heavily on an alliance with established elite groups in Indian society — landowners; the "princes" who governed large parts of the region; and the Brahmins, the highest-ranking segment of India's caste-based society. These alliances strengthened or hardened elements of "traditional" India and brought them under British control. At the same time, colonial rule changed India in a hundred ways. Its schools gave rise to a class of Western-educated and English-speaking Indians; its economic and cultural policies fostered rebellion in the rural areas; its railroads, telegraphs, and postal services linked India more closely together; its racism provoked a growing sense of an all-Indian identity; its efforts to define, and thus control, India's enormously diverse population contributed to a growing divide between its Hindu and Muslim communities.

This collection begins with a group of images that evoke familiar features of British colonial rule in India, followed by a series of documents that present a range of Indian responses to the colonial experience.

Source 18.1
Images of Colonial Rule

The British colonial presence in India has been recorded in a plethora of artistic representations. The four images that follow provide a highly selective glimpse at several features of that experience.

Questions to consider as you examine the sources:

- What does each of these images convey to you about colonial India?

- How might each of these scenes have been experienced by both British and Indian participants?

- What kinds of interactions between rulers and ruled are suggested in these images?

Source 18.1A
A British Breakfast in India

From *Anglo Indians*, engraved by J. Bouvier, 1842/Private Collection/The Stapleton Collection/Bridgeman Images

British officials and their families sought to re-create as much of English life as possible in the very different environment of India and to maintain a sharp separation between themselves and Indians. In what ways does this engraving, published in 1842, suggest that effort?

Source 18.1B
Tiger Hunting in Colonial India

A favorite sport among British colonial elites and tourists, tiger hunting served to display Victorian era "manliness," "a virile, muscular, patriotic sense of endurance." It also suggested the invincibility of the colonial state in triumphing over such a savage beast as well as its benevolence in ridding villages of their "man-eating tigers."[1]

Source 18.1C
The British and Indian Princes

In many parts of colonial India, the British governed indirectly, through traditional authorities known as "princes." Here Prince Mahadaji Sindhia entertains two British military officers at a traditional Indian nautch, or dance concert, performed by professional Indian dancing girls around 1820. Stylistically it differs from the other images in this selection because it was created by an Indian artist rather than a British one. What does this image suggest about British efforts to relate to Indian elites and Indian culture?

Source 18.1D
Blowing from a Gun

Blowing mutinous Sepoys from the guns, from "The History of the Indian Mutiny," published in 1858 (engraving), English School (19th century)/Private Collection/Ken Welsh/Bridgeman Images

Following Mughal precedents, the British frequently employed a particularly horrific form of public execution for rebels by tying the victim, or sometimes several victims, to the mouth of a cannon and then firing it. This practice was used quite extensively during the Indian uprising of 1857–1858, as illustrated in this image. The British argued that it served as a deterrent to rebellion, was more humane than the earlier Mughal practice of "flogging to death," and allowed high-caste rebels to avoid the disgrace of being polluted by contact with the untouchables who often conducted hangings. For the families of the victims, both Muslim and Hindu, it proved almost impossible to perform proper funeral and burial rites. The practice was used as late as 1871, but then was discontinued.

Source 18.2
Seeking Western Education

Indian understanding of and responses to British rule varied widely and changed over time, involving gratitude, acceptance, disappointment with unfulfilled promise, active resistance, and sharp criticism of many kinds. Sources 18.2 through 18.5 provide four examples, covering almost a hundred years, from the early nineteenth century to the early twentieth.

The first comes from Ram Mohan Roy (1772–1833). Born and highly educated within a Brahmin Hindu family, he subsequently studied both Arabic and Persian, learned English, came into contact with British Christian missionaries, and found employment with the British East India Company. He emerged in the early nineteenth century as a leading advocate for religious and social reform within India, with a particular interest in ending *sati*, the practice in which widows burned themselves on their husbands' funeral pyres. In 1823, he learned about a British plan to establish a school in Calcutta that was to focus on Sanskrit texts and traditional Hindu learning. Source 18.2 records his response to that school, and to British colonial rule, in a letter to the British governor-general of India.

Questions to consider as you examine the source:

■ Why was Roy opposed to the creation of this school?

■ What does this letter reveal about Roy's attitude toward Indian and European cultures?

■ How would you describe Roy's attitude toward British colonial rule in India?

RAM MOHAN ROY
Letter to Lord Amherst
1823

The establishment of a new Sanskrit School in Calcutta evinces the laudable desire of Government to improve the natives of India by education, a blessing for which they must ever be grateful.... When this seminary of learning was proposed ... we were filled with sanguine hopes that [it would employ] European gentlemen of talent and education to instruct the natives of India in Mathematics, Natural Philosophy, Chemistry, Anatomy, and other useful sciences, which the natives of Europe have carried to a degree of perfection that has raised them above the inhabitants of other parts of the world.... Our hearts were filled with mingled feelings of delight and gratitude; we already offered up thanks to Providence for inspiring the most generous and enlightened nations of the West with the glorious ambition of planting in Asia the arts and sciences of Modern Europe.

We find [however] that the Government are establishing a Sanskrit school under Hindu Pandits [scholars] to impart such knowledge as is already current in India. This seminary can only be expected to load the minds of youth with grammatical niceties and metaphysical distinctions of little or no practical use to the possessors or to society. The pupils will there acquire what was known two thousand years ago with the addition of vain and empty subtleties since then produced by speculative men, such as is already commonly taught in all parts of India. . . .

Neither can much improvement arise from such speculations as the following which are the themes suggested by the Vedanta [a branch of Hindu philosophy]: in what manner is the soul absorbed in the Deity? What relation does it bear to the Divine Essence? Nor will youths be fitted to be better members of society by the Vedantic doctrines which teach them to believe that all visible things have no real existence, that as father, brother, etc., have no actual entity, they consequently deserve no real affection, and therefore the sooner we escape from them and leave the world the better. . . .

[T]he Sanskrit system of education would be the best calculated to keep this country in darkness, if such had been the policy of the British legislature. But as the improvement of the native population is the object of the Government, it will consequently promote a more liberal and enlightened system of instruction, embracing Mathematics, Natural Philosophy, Chemistry, Anatomy, with other useful sciences, which may be accomplished with the sums proposed by employing a few gentlemen of talent and learning educated in Europe and providing a College furnished with necessary books, instruments, and other apparatus. In presenting this subject to your Lordship, I conceive myself discharging a solemn duty which I owe to my countrymen, and also to that enlightened sovereign and legislature which have extended their benevolent care to this distant land, actuated by a desire to improve the inhabitants, and therefore humbly trust you will excuse the liberty I have taken in thus expressing my sentiments to your Lordship.

Source: Rammohun Roy, *The English Works of Raja Rammohun Roy* (Allahabad, India: Panini Office, 1906), 471–74.

Source 18.3
The Indian Rebellion

In 1857–1858, British-ruled India erupted in violent rebellion. Some among the rebels imagined that the Mughal Empire might be restored to its former power and glory. Such was the hope that animated the Azamgarh Proclamation, issued in the summer of 1857, allegedly by the grandson of the last and largely powerless Mughal emperor, Bahadur Shah.

Questions to consider as you examine the source:

■ What grievances against British rule does this document disclose?

■ How does the proclamation imagine the future of India, should the rebellion succeed? How does this compare to Ram Mohan Roy's vision of India's future in Source 18.2?

■ To what groups or classes of people was the proclamation directed? What groups were left out in the call to rebellion? Why might they have been omitted?

PRINCE FEROZE SHAH

The Azamgarh Proclamation
1857

It is well known to all that in this age the people of Hindustan, both Hindus and Muslims, are being ruined under the tyranny and oppression of the infidel and the treacherous English. It is therefore the bounden duty of all the wealthy people of India, especially of those who have any sort of connection with any of the Muslim royal families and are considered the pastors and masters of their people, to stake their lives and property for the well-being of the public. . . . I, who am the grandson of Bahadur Shah, have . . . come here to extirpate the infidels residing in the eastern part of the country, and to liberate and protect the poor helpless people now groaning under their iron rule. . . .

Section I: Regarding Zamindars [large landowners]

It is evident the British government, in making [land] settlements, have imposed exorbitant jummas [taxes], and have disgraced and ruined several zamindars, by putting up their estates to public auction for arrears of rent, insomuch, that on the institution of a suit by a common ryot [peasant farmer] yet, a maidservant, or a slave, the respectable zamindars are summoned into court, arrested, put in gaol, and disgraced. . . . Besides this, the coffers of the zamindars are annually taxed with subscriptions for schools, hospitals, roads, etc. Such extortions will have no manner of existence in the Badshahi [restored Mughal] government; but, on the contrary, the jummas will be light, the dignity and honour of the zamindars safe, and every zamindar will have absolute rule in his own zamindary.

Section II: Regarding Merchants

It is plain that the infidel and treacherous British government have monopolized the trade of all the fine and valuable merchandise such as indigo, cloth, and other articles of shipping, leaving only the trade of trifles to the people, and even in this they are not without their share of the profits, which they secure by means of customs and stamp fees, etc., in money suits, so that the people have merely a trade in name. Besides this, the profits of the traders are taxed with postages, tolls, and subscriptions for schools. Notwithstanding all these concessions, the merchants are liable to imprisonment and disgrace at the instance or complaint of a worthless man. When the Badshahi government is established, all these aforesaid fraudulent practices shall be dispensed with, and the trade of every article, without exception both by land and water, shall be open to the native merchants of India, who will have the benefit of the government steam-vessels and steam carriages for the conveyance of their merchandise gratis. . . .

Section III: Regarding Public Servants

It is not a secret thing, that under the British government, natives employed in the civil and military services have little respect, low pay, and no manner of influence; and all the posts of dignity and emolument in both the departments are exclusively bestowed upon Englishmen. . . . But under the Badshahi government, [these] posts . . . will be given to the natives. . . . Natives, whether Hindus or Muslims, who fall fighting against the English, are sure to go to heaven; and those killed fighting for the English, will, doubtless, go to hell; therefore, all the natives in the British service ought to be alive to their religion and interest, and, abjuring their loyalty to the English, side with the Badshahi government and obtain salaries of 200 or 300 rupees per month for the present, and be entitled to high posts in future.

Section IV: Regarding Artisans

It is evident that the Europeans, by the introduction of English articles into India, have thrown the weavers, the cotton-dressers, the carpenters, the blacksmiths, and the shoemakers, etc., out of employ, and have engrossed their occupations, so that every description of native artisan has been reduced to beggary. But under the Badshahi government the native artisan will exclusively be employed in the services of the kings, the rajahas, and the rich; and this will no doubt insure their prosperity.

Section V: Regarding Pundits [scholars], Fakirs [religious mystics], and Other Learned Persons

The pundits and fakirs being the guardians of the Hindu and Muslim religions, respectively, and the European being the enemies of both the religions, and as at present a war is raging against the English on account of religion, the pundits and fakirs are bound to present themselves to me and take their share in the holy war, otherwise they will stand condemned . . . but if they come, they will, when the Badshahi government is well established, receive rent-free lands.

Lastly, be it known to all, that whoever out of the above-named classes, shall . . . still cling to the British government, all his estates shall be confiscated, and his property plundered, and he himself, with his whole family, shall be imprisoned, and ultimately put to death.

Source: "The Azamgarh Proclamation," *Delhi Gazette*, September 29, 1857.

Source 18.4
The Credits and Debits of British Rule in India

Dadabhai Naoroji (1825–1917) was a well-educated Indian intellectual, a cotton trader in London, and a founding member of the Indian National Congress, an elite organization established in 1885 to press for a wider range of opportunities for educated Indians within the colonial system. He was also the first Indian to serve in the British Parliament. In 1871, while addressing an English audience in London, he was asked about the impact of British rule in India. Representing a "moderate" view within Indian political circles at the time, he organized his response in terms of "credits" and "debits."

Questions to consider as you examine the source:

■ According to Naoroji, what are the chief advantages and drawbacks of British rule?

■ What is Naoroji seeking from Britain?

■ How does Naoroji's posture toward British rule compare to that of Ram Mohan Roy in Source 18.2 or the Azamgarh Proclamation in Source18.3?

DADABHAI NAOROJI

Speech to a London Audience

1871

Credit

In the Cause of Humanity: Abolition of *suttee* and infanticide. Destruction of *Dacoits*, *Thugs*, *Pindarees* [various criminal groups] and other such pests of Indian society. Allowing remarriage of Hindu widows, and charitable aid in time of famine. Glorious work all this, of which any nation may well be proud. . . .

In the Cause of Civilization: Education, both male and female. Though yet only partial, an inestimable blessing as far as it has gone, and leading gradually to the destruction of superstition, and many moral and social evils. Resuscitation of India's own noble literature, modified and refined by the enlightenment of the West.

Politically: Peace and order. Freedom of speech and liberty of the press. Higher political knowledge and aspirations. Improvement of government in the native states. Security of life and property. Freedom from oppression caused by the caprice or greed of despotic rulers, and from devastation by war. Equal justice between man and man (sometimes vitiated by partiality to Europeans). Services of highly educated administrators, who have achieved the abovementioned results.

Materially: Loans for railways and irrigation. Development of a few valuable products, such as indigo, tea, coffee, silk, etc. Increase of exports. Telegraphs.

Generally: A slowly growing desire of late to treat India equitably, and as a country held in trust. Good intentions. No nation on the face of the earth has ever had the opportunity of achieving such a glorious work as this. . . . I appreciate, and so do my countrymen, what England has done for India, and I know that it is only in British hands that her regeneration can be accomplished. Now for the debit side.

Debit

In the Cause of Humanity: Nothing. Everything, therefore, is in your favor under this heading.

In the Cause of Civilization: As I have said already, there has been a failure to do as much as might have been done, but I put nothing to the debit. Much has been done, though.

Politically: Repeated breach of pledges to give the natives a fair and reasonable share in the higher administration of their own country, which has much shaken confidence in the good faith of the British word. Political aspirations and the legitimate claim to have a reasonable voice in the legislation and the imposition and disbursement of taxes, met to a very slight degree, thus treating the natives of India not as British subjects, in whom representation is a birthright. Consequent on the above, an utter disregard of the feelings and views of the natives. . . .

Financially: All attention is engrossed in devising new modes of taxation, without any adequate effort to increase the means of the people to pay; and the consequent vexation and oppressiveness of the taxes imposed, imperial and local. Inequitable financial relations between England and India, i.e., the political debt of £100,000,000 clapped on India's shoulders, and all home charges also, though the British Exchequer contributes nearly £3,000,000 to the expense of the colonies.

Materially: The political drain, up to this time, from India to England, of above £500,000,000, at the lowest computation, in principal alone, which with interest would be some thousands of millions. The further continuation of this drain at the rate, at present, of above £12,000,000 per annum, with a tendency to increase. The consequent continuous impoverishment and exhaustion of the country, except so far as it has been very partially relieved and replenished by the railway and irrigation loans, and the windfall of the consequences of the American war, since 1850. Even with this relief, the material condition of India is such that the great mass of the poor have hardly tuppence a day and a few rags, or a scanty subsistence. The famines that were in their power to prevent, if they had done their duty, as a good and intelligent government. The policy adopted during the last fifteen years of building railways, irrigation works, etc., is hopeful, has already resulted in much good to your credit, and if persevered in, gratitude and contentment will follow. An increase of exports without adequate compensation; loss of manufacturing industry and skill. Here I end the debit side.

Summary

To sum up the whole, the British rule has been: morally, a great blessing; politically, peace and order on one hand, blunders on the other; materially, impoverishment, relieved as far as the railway and other loans go. The natives call the British system "Sakar ki Churi," the knife of sugar. That is to say, there is no oppression, it is all smooth and sweet, but it is the knife, notwithstanding. I mention this that you should know these feelings. Our great misfortune is that you do not know our wants. When you will know our real wishes, I have not the least doubt that you would do justice. The genius and spirit of the British people is fair play and justice.

Source: Dadabhai Naoroji, *Essays, Speeches, Addresses and Writings* (Bombay: Caxton Printing Works, 1887), 131–36.

Source 18.5
Gandhi on Modern Civilization

Mahatma Gandhi (1869–1948), clearly modern India's most beloved leader, is best known for his theories of *satyagraha*. This was an aggressive but nonviolent approach to political action that directly challenged and disobeyed unjust laws, while seeking to change the hearts of India's British oppressors. But Gandhi's thinking was distinctive in another way as well, for he objected not only to the foreign and exploitative character of British rule, but also, more fundamentally, to the modern civilization that it carried. In 1909, he spelled out that critique in a pamphlet titled *Hind Swaraj* (*Indian Home Rule*). There Gandhi assumes the role of an "editor," responding to questions from a "reader."

Questions to consider as you examine the source:

- What is Gandhi's most fundamental criticism of British rule in India?

- What is the difference between his concept of "civilization" and that which he ascribes to the British?

- What kind of future does Gandhi seek for his country?

MAHATMA GANDHI

Indian Home Rule

1909

READER: Now you will have to explain what you mean by civilization.

EDITOR: Let us first consider what state of things is described by the word "civilization." . . . The people of Europe today live in better-built houses than they did a hundred years ago. This is considered an emblem of civilization. . . . If people of a certain country, who have hitherto not been in the habit of wearing much clothing, boots, etc., adopt European clothing, they are supposed to have become civilized out of savagery. Formerly, in Europe, people ploughed their lands mainly by manual labor. Now, one man can plough a vast tract by means of steam engines and can thus amass great wealth. This is called a sign of civilization. Formerly, only a few men wrote valuable books. Now, anybody writes and prints anything he likes and poisons people's minds. Formerly, men traveled in wagons. Now, they fly through the air in trains at the rate of four hundred and more miles per day. This is considered the height of civilization. It has been stated that, as men progress, they shall be able to travel in airship and reach any part of the world in a few hours. . . . Everything will be done by machinery. Formerly, when people wanted to fight with one another, they measured between them their bodily strength; now it is possible to take away thousands of lives by one man working behind a gun from a hill. This is civilization. . . . Formerly, men were made slaves under physical compulsion. Now they are enslaved by temptation of money and of the luxuries that money can buy. . . . This civilization takes note neither of morality nor of religion. Its votaries calmly state that their business is not to teach religion. Some even consider it to be a superstitious growth. . . . This civilization is irreligion, and it has taken such a hold on the people in Europe that those who are in it appear to be half mad. They lack real physical strength or courage. They keep up their energy by intoxication. They can hardly be happy in solitude. Women, who should be the queens of households, wander in the streets or they slave away in factories. For the sake of a pittance, half a million women in England alone are laboring under trying circumstances in factories or similar institutions.

This civilization is such that one has only to be patient and it will be self-destroyed. . . . I cannot give you an adequate conception of it. It is eating into the vitals of the English nation. It must be shunned. . . . Civilization is not an incurable disease, but it should never be forgotten that the English are at present afflicted by it.

READER: I now understand why the English hold India. I should like to know your views about the condition of our country.

EDITOR: It is a sad condition. . . . It is my deliberate opinion that India is being ground down, not under the English heel, but under that of modern civilization. It is groaning under the monster's terrible weight. [M]y first complaint is that India is becoming irreligious. . . . We are turning away from God. . . . [W]e should set a limit to our worldly ambition. . . . [O]ur religious ambition should be illimitable. . . .

EDITOR: Railways, lawyers, and doctors have impoverished the country so much so that, if we do not wake up in time, we shall be ruined.

READER: I do now, indeed, fear that we are not likely to agree at all. You are attacking the very institutions which we have hitherto considered to be good.

EDITOR: It must be manifest to you that, but for the railways, the English could not have such a hold on India as they have. The railways, too, have spread the bubonic plague. Without them the masses could not move from place to place. They are the carriers of plague germs. Formerly we had natural segregation. Railways have also increased the frequency of famines because, owing to facility of means of locomotion, people sell out their grain and it is sent to the dearest markets. People become careless and so the pressure of famine increases. Railways accentuate the evil nature of man. Bad men fulfill their evil designs with greater rapidity. . . .

READER: You have denounced railways, lawyers, and doctors. I can see that you will discard all machinery. What, then, is civilization?

EDITOR: The answer to that question is not difficult. I believe that the civilization India has evolved is not to be beaten in the world. . . . India is still, somehow or other, sound at the foundation. . . . India remains immovable and that is her glory. It is a charge against India that her people are so uncivilized, ignorant, and stolid that it is not possible to induce them to adopt any changes. It is a charge really against our merit. What we have tested and found true on the anvil of experience, we dare not change. Many thrust their advice upon India, and she remains steady. This is her beauty: it is the sheet-anchor of our hope.

Civilization is that mode of conduct which points out to man the path of duty. Performance of duty and observance of morality are convertible terms. To observe morality is to attain mastery over our mind and our passions. So doing, we know ourselves. . . . If this definition be correct, then India . . . has nothing to learn from anybody else. . . . Our ancestors, therefore, set a limit to our indulgences. [They] dissuaded us from luxuries and pleasures. We have managed with the same kind of plough as existed thousands of years ago. We have retained the same kind of cottages that we had in former times and our indigenous education remains the same as before. We have had no system of life-corroding competition. Each followed his own occupation or trade and charged a regulation wage. It was not that we did not know how to invent machinery, but our forefathers knew that, if we set our hearts after such things, we would become slaves and lose our moral fiber. . . . They were, therefore, satisfied with small villages. . . . A nation with a constitution like this is fitter to teach others than to learn from others. . . .

The tendency of the Indian civilization is to elevate the moral being; that of the Western civilization is to propagate immorality. The latter is godless; the former is based on a belief in God. So understanding and so believing, it behooves every lover of India to cling to the Indian civilization even as a child clings to the mother's breast.

Source: Mohandas Gandhi, *Indian Home Rule* (Madras: Ganesh, 1922), pts. 6, 8, 9, 10, 13.

ESSAY QUESTIONS

Colonial India: Experience and Response

1. **Describing alternative futures:** What can you infer about the kind of future for India that the authors or creators of these sources anticipate?

2. **Assessing change through time:** In what ways did understandings of British colonial rule change over time? How might you account for these changes?

3. **Considering visual and written sources:** How do these visual and written sources differ in terms of the understanding they convey about British India?

4. **Noticing what's missing:** What voices are not represented in these sources? How might such people have articulated a different understanding of the colonial experience?

5. **Responding to Gandhi:** How might each of the other authors or artists have responded to Gandhi's analysis of British colonial role and his understanding of "civilization"? To what extent do you find Gandhi's views relevant to the conditions of the early twenty-first century?

Note

1. Kevin Hannam and Anya Diekmann, *Tourism and India: A Critical Introduction* (New York: Routledge, 2011), 69–70.

CHAPTER 19

THINKING THROUGH SOURCES

Japan and the West in the Nineteenth Century

During the nineteenth century, Japan's relationship with the West changed profoundly in a pattern that included sharp antagonism, enthusiastic embrace, selective borrowing, and equality on the international stage. At the time, that changing relationship had implications as well for China, Korea, Russia, and elsewhere, even as it laid the foundation for twentieth-century global conflict in World War II.

In the initial decades of the nineteenth century, the Western world was increasingly impinging upon Japan, which had closed itself off from Europe and America since the early seventeenth century with the exception of a small Dutch trading port near Nagasaki. But then a number of Western whaling ships had penetrated Japanese waters, and suspicions rose. Aizawa Seishisai, a prominent Japanese Confucian scholar, gave voice to these worries in 1825:

> The barbarians live ten thousand miles across the sea; when they set off on foreign conquests, they must procure supplies and provisions from the enemy. That is why they trade and fish. Their men of war are self-sufficient away from home. If their only motive for harpooning whales was to obtain whale meat, they could do so in their own waters. Why should they risk long, difficult voyages just to harpoon whales in eastern seas? Their ships can be outfitted for trading, or fishing, or fighting. Can anyone guarantee that their merchant vessels and fishing boats of today will not turn into warships tomorrow?[1]

Source 19.1
Continuing Japanese Isolation

In response to concerns about Western intervention, the Japanese government, known as the Tokugawa shogunate, issued an edict that reiterated in the strongest possible terms the country's long-standing posture of isolation from the West.

Questions to consider as you examine the source:

■ What understanding of the West did this edict reflect?

■ What actions did the edict prescribe?

■ Why might Westerners find the policy offensive and unacceptable?

An Edict of Expulsion
1825

We have issued instructions on how to deal with foreign ships on numerous occasions up to the present. In the Bunka era [1804–1817] we issued new edicts to deal with Russian ships. But a few years ago a British ship wreaked havoc in Nagasaki, and more recently their rowboats have been landing to procure firewood, water, and provisions. Two years ago they forced their way ashore, stole livestock and extorted rice. Thus they have become steadily more unruly, and moreover seem to be propagating their wicked religion among our people. This situation plainly cannot be left to itself.

All Southern Barbarians and Westerners, not only the English, worship Christianity, that wicked cult prohibited in our land. Henceforth, whenever a foreign ship is sighted approaching any point on our coast, all persons on hand should fire on and drive it off. If the vessel heads for the open sea, you need not pursue it; allow it to escape. If the foreigners force their way ashore, you may capture and incarcerate them, and if their mother ship approaches, you may destroy it as circumstances dictate.

Note that Chinese, Korean, and Ryukyuans [people from a group of islands south of Japan] can be differentiated [from Westerners] by the physiognomy and ship design, but Dutch ships are indistinguishable [from those of other Westerners]. Even so, have no compunctions about firing on [the Dutch] by mistake; when in doubt, drive the ship away without hesitation. Never be caught offguard.

Source: Bob Tadashi Wakabayashi, *Anti-Foreignism and Western Learning in Early-Modern Japan* (Cambridge: Harvard University Press, 1985), 60.

Source 19.2
The Debate: Expel the Barbarians

The arrival of United States admiral Matthew Perry in 1853, demanding that the country open to foreign commerce and navigation, brought to a head the question of Japan's isolationist policy and prompted a considerable debate in Japanese circles. Advocating forceful expulsion of the Americans and sharply opposing any treaty with them was Tokugawa Nariaki, the *daimyo*, or ruler, of a domain on the eastern coast of Japan.

Questions to consider as you examine the source:

■ What were Tokugawa Nariaki's arguments for a policy of war?

■ What did he fear if Japan tried to accommodate Perry's demands?

TOKUGAWA NARIAKI

Memorial on the American Demand for a Treaty

1853

It is my belief that the first and most urgent of our tasks is for the Bakufu [government of the shogun] to make its choice between peace and war. . . . [I]f we put our trust in war, the whole country's morale will be increased and even if we sustain an initial defeat, we will in the end expel the foreigner. . . . [W]e must never choose the policy of peace. . . .

Although our country's territory is not extensive, foreigners both fear and respect us. That, after all, is because our resoluteness and military prowess have been clearly demonstrated to the world. . . . Despite this, the Americans who arrived recently, though fully aware of the Bakufu's prohibition, entered Uraga displaying a white flag as a symbol of peace and insisted on presenting their written request. Moreover they entered Edo Bay, fired heavy guns in salute and even went so far as to conduct surveys without permission. They were arrogant and discourteous, their actions an outrage. Indeed, this was the greatest disgrace we have suffered since the dawn of our history. . . . The foreigners, having thus ignored our prohibition and penetrated our waters even to the vicinity of the capital, threatening us and making demands upon us, should it happen not only the Bakufu fails to expel them but also that it concludes an agreement in accordance with their requests, then I fear it would be impossible to maintain our national prestige.

The prohibition of Christianity is the first rule of the Tokugawa [government]. . . . The Bakufu can never ignore or overlook the evils of Christianity. Yet if the Americans are allowed to come again this religion will inevitably raise its head once more, however strict the prohibition and this, I fear, is something we could never justify to the spirits of our ancestors.

To exchange our valuable articles like gold, silver, copper, and iron for useless foreign goods like woolens and satin is to incur great loss while acquiring not the smallest benefit. . . .

For some years Russia, England, and others have sought trade with us, but the Bakufu has not permitted it. Should permission be granted to the Americans, on what ground would it be possible to refuse if Russia and the others [again] request it?

It is widely stated that [apart from trade] the foreigners have no other evil designs and that if only the Bakufu will permit trade there will be no further difficulty. However, it is their practice first to seek a foothold by means of trade and then to go on to propagate Christianity and make other unreasonable demands. Thus we would be repeating the blunders of others . . . and more recently in the Opium War in China.

[I]f the people of Japan stand firmly united, if we complete our military preparations and return to the state of society that existed before the middle ages [when the emperor ruled the country directly], then we will even be able to go out against foreign countries and spread abroad our fame and prestige. But if we open trade at the demand of the foreigners, for no better reason than that, our habits today being those of peace and indolence, men have shown fear merely at the coming of a handful of foreign warships, then it would truly be a vain illusion to think of evolving any long-range plan for going out against foreign countries.

I hear that all, even though they be commoners, who have witnessed the recent actions of the foreigners, think them abominable. Since even ignorant commoners are talking in this way, I fear that if the Bakufu does not decide to carry out expulsion, if its handling of the matter shows nothing but excess of leniency and appeasement of the foreigners, then the lower orders may fail to understand its ideas and hence opposition might arise from evil men who have lost their respect for Bakufu authority. . . .

[I]f the Bakufu, now and henceforward, shows itself resolute for expulsion, the immediate effect will be to increase ten-fold the morale of the country . . . only by so doing will the shogun be able to fulfill his "barbarian-expelling" duty and unite the men of every province in carrying out their proper military functions. . . .

In these feeble days men tend to cling to peace; they are not fond of defending their country by war. They slander those of us who are determined to fight, calling us lovers of war, men who enjoy conflict. If matters become desperate they might, in their enormous folly, try to overthrow those of us who are determined to fight, offering excuses to the enemy and concluding a peace agreement with him. They would thus in the end bring total destruction upon us.

Source: *Selected Documents on Japanese Foreign Policy*, translated by Beasley (1955), 778w from pp.102–107. By permission of Oxford University Press.

Source 19.3
The Debate: A Sumo Wrestler and a Foreigner

The debate about Japan's response to Perry's demands not only engaged political and intellectual elites, but found expression as well in the popular media of woodblock prints. In 1861, such a print showed a Japanese sumo wrestler tossing a boastful French competitor. The inscription reads: "Hershan, wrestler without peer, comes from Calais in France, a part of Europe. He has traveled to the countries of the world, and nowhere has he been defeated. He is very boastful and came to our country to Yokohama and asked for a match. To the glory of Japan, a Japanese sumo wrestler threw him to the ground."[2]

Questions to consider as you examine the source:

- Why might this image carry considerable appeal in the middle of a national debate about how to deal with the intrusive foreigners?

- In what ways could it be seen as a visual depiction of Tokugawa Nariaki's point of view?

- What does the inscription add to your understanding of the image?

A Sumo Wrestler and a Foreigner

Yoshiku Utagawa (1833–1904), *Sumo Wrestler Tossing a Foreigner*, 1st month, 1861. Polychrome woodblock print; inks and colors on paper. Image: 14¼ × 9⅜ in. (36.2 × 23.8 cm.). Bequest of William S. Lieberman, 2005 (2007.49.225). The Metropolitan Museum of Art, New York, NY, USA/Image copyright © The Metropolitan Museum of Art/Image source: Art Resource, NY

Source 19.4

The Debate: Eastern Ethics and Western Science

The other side of this debate made the case for opening Japan to the West and even embracing aspects of its culture. Ii Naosuke, another *daimyo* and a bitter opponent of Tokugawa Nariaki, wrote in 1853:

> It is impossible in the crisis we now face to ensure the safety and tranquility of our country merely by an insistence on the seclusion laws as we did in former times. . . . The exchange of goods is a universal practice. This we should explain to the spirits of our ancestors. And we should tell the foreigners that we mean in future to send trading vessels to the Dutch company's factory in Batavia to engage in trade. . . . As we increase the number of our ships and our mastery of technique, Japanese will be able to sail the oceans freely and gain direct knowledge of conditions abroad.[3]

More generally and more famously, Sakuma Shozan, a Confucian-educated official in the shogun's government, argued that Japan must combine Eastern Confucian-oriented ethics and Western science. He had been briefly imprisoned in 1854 for encouraging one of his students to stow away on one of Perry's ships in order to learn something of Western ways. Shortly after his release, he wrote his famous work, *Reflections on My Errors*. It was not really an apology for his actions, but a defense of his position.

Questions to consider as you examine the source:

■ How do you understand the metaphor in the first paragraph of this excerpt about "giv[ing] the medicine secretly"?

■ What departures from existing practices does Sakuma Shozan advocate? In what ways is he critical of Japan's military and intellectual leaders?

■ On what issues might Sakuma Shozan and Tokugawa Nariaki agree? How could you define their differences?

SAKUMA SHOZAN

Reflections on My Errors

Mid-1850s

Take, for example, a man who is grieved by the illness of his lord or his father, and who is seeking medicine to cure it. If he is fortunate enough to secure the medicine, and is certain that it will be efficacious, then, certainly, without questioning either its cost or the quality of its name, he will beg his lord or father to take it. Should the latter refuse on the grounds that he dislikes the name, does the younger man make various schemes to give the medicine secretly, or does he simply sit by and wait for his master to die? There is no question about it: . . . the feeling of genuine sincerity and heartfelt grief on the part of the subject or son makes it absolutely impossible for him to sit idly and watch his master's anguish; consequently, even if he knows that he will later have to face his master's anger, he cannot but give the medicine secretly. . . .

The gentleman has five pleasures, but wealth and rank are not among them. That his house understands decorum and righteousness and remains free from family rifts — this is one pleasure. That exercising care in giving to and taking from others, he provides for himself honestly, free, internally, from shame before his wife and children, and externally, from disgrace before the public — this is the second pleasure. That he expounds and glorifies the learning of the sages, knows in his heart the great Way, and in all situations contents himself with his duty, in adversity as well as in prosperity — this is the third pleasure. . . . That he is born after the opening of the vistas of science by the Westerners, and can therefore understand principles not known to the sages and wise men of old — this is the fourth pleasure. That he employs the ethics of the East and the scientific technique of the West, neglecting neither the spiritual nor material aspects of life, combining subjective and objective, and thus bringing benefit to the people and serving the nation — this is the fifth pleasure. . . .

The principal requisite of national defense is that it prevents the foreign barbarians from holding us in contempt. The existing coastal defense installations all lack method; the pieces of artillery that have been set up are improperly made; and the officials who negotiate with the foreigners are mediocrities who have no understanding of warfare. The situation being such, even though we wish to avoid incurring the scorn of the barbarians, how, in fact, can we do so? . . .

Of the men who now hold posts as commanders of the army, those who are not dukes or princes or men of noble rank, are members of wealthy families. As such, they find their daily pleasure in drinking wine, singing, and dancing; and they are ignorant of military strategy and discipline. Should a national emergency arise, there is no one who could command the respect of the warriors and halt the enemy's attack. This is the great sorrow of our times. For this reason, I have wished to follow in substance the Western principles of armament, and, by banding together loyal, valorous, strong men of old, established families not in the military class — men of whom one would be equal to ten ordinary men — to form a voluntary group which would be made to have as its sole aim that of guarding the nation and protecting the people. Anyone wishing to join the society would be tested and his merits examined; and, if he did not shirk hardship, he would then be permitted to join. Men of talent in military strategy, planning, and administration would be advanced to positions of leadership, and then, if the day should come when the country must be defended, this group could be gathered together and organized into an army to await official commands. It is to be hoped that they would drive the enemy away and perform greater service than those who now form the military class. . . .

Mathematics is the basis for all learning. In the Western world after this science was discovered military tactics advanced greatly. . . . At the present time, if we wish really to complete our military preparations, we must develop this branch of study. . . .

What do the so-called scholars of today actually do? Do they clearly and tacitly understand the way in which the gods and sages established this nation, or the way in which Yao, Shun, and the divine emperors of the three dynasties governed? Do they, after having learned the rites and music, punishment and administration, the classics and governmental system, go on to discuss and learn the elements of the art of war, of military discipline, of the principles of machinery? Do they make exhaustive studies of conditions in foreign countries? Of effective defense methods? Of strategy in setting up strongholds, defense barriers, and reinforcements? Of the knowledge of computation, gravitation, geometry, and mathematics? If they do, I have not heard of it!

Therefore I ask what the so-called scholars of today actually do. . . .

In order to master the barbarians there is nothing so effective as to ascertain in the beginning conditions among them. To do this, there is no better first step than to be familiar with barbarian tongues. Thus, learning a barbarian language is not only a step toward knowing the barbarians, but also the groundwork for mastering them.

Source: *Sources of Japanese Tradition*, Volume Two, compiled by William De Bary et al. Copyright © 2001 Columbia University Press. Reprinted with permission of the publisher.

Source 19.5
Westernization

The great debate of the 1850s and 1860s, prompted by Perry's arrival, came to an end with the Meiji Restoration of 1868. Now the shogunate was replaced by a new government, headed directly by the emperor, and committed to a more thorough transformation of the country than Sakuma Shozan had ever imagined. Particularly among the young, there was an acute awareness of the need to create a new culture that could support a revived Japan. "We have no history," declared one of these students; "our history begins today."[4] In this context, much that was Western was enthusiastically embraced. The technological side of this borrowing, contributing much to Japan's remarkable industrialization, was the most obvious expression of this westernization.

But borrowing extended as well to more purely cultural matters. Eating beef became popular, despite Buddhist objections. Many men adopted Western hairstyles and grew beards, even though the facial hair of Westerners had earlier been portrayed as ugly. In 1872, Western dress was ordered for all official ceremonies. Ballroom dancing became popular among the elite, as did Western instruments like the piano and harpsichord. Women in these circles likewise adopted Western ways, as illustrated in Source 19.5, an 1887 woodblock print titled *Illustration of Singing by the Plum Garden*. At the same time, the image also includes many traditional Japanese elements. The flowering trees in the background had long been an important subject of study in Japan's artistic tradition, and the flower arrangement on the right represents a popular Japanese art form. Moreover, the dress of the woman in the middle seems to reflect earlier Japanese court traditions that encouraged women to wear many layers of kimonos.

Questions to consider as you examine the source:

■ What elements of Western culture can you identify in this visual source?

■ In what ways does this print reflect the continuing appeal of Japanese culture? Pay attention to the scenery, the tree, and the flowers.

■ Why were so many Japanese so enamored of Western culture during this time? And why did the Japanese government so actively encourage their interest?

Women and Westernization

Singing by the Plum Garden (Baien shoka zu), Meiji Era, 1887, ink and color on paper, by Totohara Chikanobu (1838–1912)/Museum of Fine Arts, Boston, Massachusetts, USA/Gift of L. Aaron Lebowich/Bridgeman Images

Source 19.6
A Critique of Westernization

Not everyone in Japan was so enthusiastic about the adoption of Western culture, and by the late 1870s and into the next decade numerous essays and images satirized the apparently indiscriminate fascination with all things European. Source 19.6, drawn by Japanese cartoonist Honda Kinkichiro in 1879, represents that point of view. One caption that accompanied the draw-ing reads as follows: "Mr. Morse [an American zoologist who introduced

Darwin's theory of evolution to Japan in 1877] explains that all human beings were monkeys in the beginning. In the beginning — but even now aren't we still monkeys? When it comes to Western things we think the red beards are the most skillful at everything."[5] A second caption in English below the drawing further develops this theme.

Questions to consider as you examine the source:

■ What specific aspects of Japan's efforts at westernization is the artist mocking?

■ Why might the artist have used a Western scientific theory (Darwinian evolution) to criticize excessive westernization in Japan?

■ Why do you think a reaction set in against the cultural imitation of Europe?

Critique of Wholesale Westernization

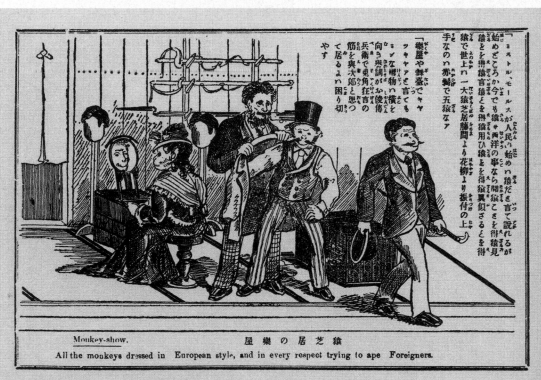

Monkey-show. 猿芝居の楽屋

All the monkeys dressed in European style, and in every respect trying to ape Foreigners.

25 猿芝居の楽屋（錦吉郎　明治12年 4 月）

Source 19.7
War and Empire

Behind Japan's modernization and westernization was the recognition that Western imperialism was surging in Asia and that China was a prime example of what happened to countries unable to defend themselves against it. Accordingly, achieving political and military equality with the Great Powers of Europe and the United States became a central aim of Japan's modernization program.

Strengthening Japan against Western aggression increasingly meant "throwing off Asia," a phrase that implied rejecting many of Japan's own cultural traditions and its habit of imitating China as well as creating an Asian empire of its own. Fukuzawa Yukichi, a popular advocate of Western knowledge, declared:

> We must not wait for neighboring countries to become civilized so that we can together promote Asia's revival. Rather we should leave their ranks and join forces with the civilized countries of the West. We don't have to give China and Korea any special treatment just because they are neighboring countries. We should deal with them as Western people do. . . . I reject the idea that we must continue to associate with bad friends in East Asia.[6]

Historically the Japanese had borrowed a great deal from China — Buddhism, Confucianism, court rituals, city-planning ideas, administrative traditions, and elements of the Chinese script. But Japan's victory in a war with China in 1894–1895 showed clearly that it had thrown off the country in whose cultural shadow it had lived for centuries. Furthermore, Japan had begun to acquire an East Asian empire in Korea and Taiwan at the expense of China. Even more dramatically, its triumph over Russia in 1904–1905 illustrated its ability to stand up even to a major European power. It was the first modern military victory by an Asian country against a Western power, and its implications resonated widely.

The significance of that victory is expressed in Source 19.7, a 1904 print by Japanese artist Chomatsu Tomisato, created during the Russo-Japanese War. It shows a triumphant Japan, stomping on a Russian battleship and holding aloft a figure representing the Russian czar Nicholas, who carries a white flag of surrender. Korea cowers behind the Japanese figure, while China kneels in submission.

Questions to consider as you examine the source:

- What overall message did the artist seek to convey in this print? How might you describe the Japanese view of the world that it expresses?

- What do the images of China and Korea evoke?

- How would you describe the posture of Turkey (Tolky), the various European powers, and the United States in this image? Notice that several of them are carrying the Japanese flag.

War and Empire

Source 19.8
Japan in the Early Twentieth Century

Early in the new century, a prominent Japanese political figure, Okuma Shigenobu, summed up his view of the country's transformation over the past half century.

Questions to consider as you examine the source:

■ What were the greatest sources of pride to Okuma?

■ To what did he attribute his country's progress?

■ In his view, what elements of Japanese tradition were maintained amid all the changes?

■ What groups of people might challenge Okuma's description of Japan, and how would they do it?

OKUMA SHIGENOBU
Fifty Years of New Japan
1907–1908

By comparing the Japan of fifty years ago with the Japan of today, it will be seen that she has gained considerably in the extent of her territory, as well as in her population, which now numbers nearly fifty million. Her government has become constitutional not only in name, but in fact, and her national education has attained to a high degree of excellence. In commerce and industry, the emblems of peace, she has also made rapid strides, until her import and export trades together amounted in 1907 to the enormous sum of 926,000,000 yen. . . . Her general progress, during the short space of half a century, has been so sudden and swift that it presents a rare spectacle in the history of the world.

This leap forward is the result of the stimulus which the country received on coming into contact with the civilization of Europe and America, and may well, in its broad sense, be regarded as a boon conferred by foreign intercourse. Foreign intercourse it was that animated the national consciousness of our people, who under the feudal system lived localized and disunited, and foreign intercourse it is that has enabled Japan to stand up as a world power. We possess today a powerful army and navy, but it was after Western models that we laid their foundations by establishing a system of conscription in pursuance of the principle "all our sons are soldiers," by promoting military education, and by encouraging the manufacture of arms and the art of shipbuilding. We have reorganized the systems of central and local administration, and effected reforms in the educational system of the empire. All this is nothing but the result of adopting the superior features of Western institutions. That Japan has been enabled to do so is a boon conferred on her by foreign intercourse, and it may be said that the nation has succeeded in this grand metamorphosis through the promptings and the influence of foreign civilization. . . .

For twenty centuries the nation has drunk freely of the civilizations of Korea, China, . . . yet we remain today politically unaltered under one Imperial House and sovereign, that has descended in an unbroken line for a length of time absolutely unexampled in the world. . . .

They [the Japanese people] have welcomed Occidental civilization while preserving their old Oriental civilization. They have attached great importance to Bushido [the samurai way of life], and at the same time held in the highest respect the spirit of charity and humanity. They have ever made a point of choosing the middle course in everything, and have aimed at being always well-balanced. . . . We are conservative simultaneously with being progressive; we are aristocratic and at the same time democratic; we are individualistic while also being socialistic. In these respects we may be said to somewhat resemble the Anglo-Saxon race.

Source: Count Segenobu Okuma, *Fifty Years of New Japan*, English version edited by Marcus Huish, vol. 2 (London: Smith, Elder & Co., 1909), 554–55, 571–72.

ESSAY QUESTIONS

Japan and the West in the Nineteenth Century

1. **Explaining change:** How and why had Japanese perceptions of themselves and their relationship to the West changed during the nineteenth and early twentieth centuries? What elements of continuity in Japanese traditions are evident in these sources?

2. **Making comparisons:** Based on these sources and the documents in Working with Evidence: Changing China in Chapter 19, how might you compare Japanese and Chinese perceptions of the West during the nineteenth century? What accounts for both the similarities and differences?

3. **Distinguishing modernization and westernization:** Based on a careful reading of Chapter 19, including the documents and images, do you think that technological borrowing (modernization) requires cultural borrowing (westernization) as well? Was it possible during the nineteenth century to modernize while avoiding the incorporation of Western culture at the same time? What do the examples of China, the Ottoman Empire, and Japan suggest about this question?

Notes

1. Bob Tadashi Wakabayashi, *Anti-Foreignism and Western Learning in Early-Modern Japan* (Cambridge: Harvard University Press, 1985), 208–9.

2. M. William Steele, *Alternative Narratives in Modern Japanese History* (London: Routledge, 2003), 29.

3. Quoted in Peter Duus, *The Japanese Discovery of America* (Boston: Bedford/St. Martin's, 1997), 100–101.

4. Quoted in Marius B. Jansen, *The Making of Modern Japan* (Cambridge, MA: Harvard University Press, 2000), 460.

5. Quoted in Julia Meech-Pekarik, *The World of the Meiji Print: Impressions of a New Civilization* (New York: Weatherhill, 1986), 182.

6. Quoted in Oka Yoshitake, prologue to *The Emergence of Imperial Japan*, edited by Marlene Mayo (Lexington, MA: D. C. Heath, 1970).

CHAPTER 20

THINKING THROUGH SOURCES

Experiencing World War I

The history of the First World War is often told in terms of diplomatic maneuvering, international alliances, altered borders, negotiated treaties, military strategies, battles, and new technologies of war. Here, however, we set aside these important matters to focus on the experience of the Great War as reflected in the accounts of particular individuals, most of them quite ordinary and unknown beyond the circle of their families and friends. Of course, the experience of the war varied greatly. Men and women; Europeans, Asians, and Africans; officers and enlisted men; refugees and prisoners of war; pacifists and militarists — all of these and many others as well encountered the war in quite different ways. Furthermore, the enthusiasm for the war that characterized many at its beginning soon turned to horror and despair as it became apparent that the conflict would drag bloodily on for years. From this immense variety, the following sources provide just a glimpse of the powerful impact of World War I on a number of individuals.

Source 20.1
Experiences on the Battlefront

"Bombardment, barrage, curtain-fire, mines, gas, tanks, machine guns, hand grenades — words, words, but they hold the horror of the world." Such was the strained effort of German war veteran Erich Maria Remarque in his novel *All Quiet on the Western Front* to find language to describe what he and millions of others had experienced on the battlefield. The four sources that follow present individual experiences of those battlefields. Source 20.1A derives from a letter that British officer Julian Grenfell wrote to his parents, describing the early stages of trench warfare, in which lines of entrenched men, often not far apart, periodically went "over the top," only to gain a few yards of bloody ground before being thrown back with enormous casualties on both sides. Source 20.1B shows a particular instance of this process as depicted by the British painter John Nash (1893–1977), an official war artist who took part in such an operation in 1917. Only twelve men out of eighty in his unit survived the attack depicted. Source 20.1C provides a perspective from a German soldier, twenty-three-year-old Hugo Mueller, while Source 20.1D offers commentary from an Indian soldier, Behari Lal.

Questions to consider as you examine the sources:

■ What insights about the experience of fighting in World War I might you derive from these sources?

■ What do they convey about the impact of the war on the outlook of these men?

■ To what extent do these sources reveal the horrors of war in general, and in what ways do they reflect the distinctive features of World War I?

Source 20.1A
JULIAN GRENFELL

Letter from a British Officer in the Trenches
November 18, 1914

They had us out again for 48 hours [in the] trenches. . . . After the shells, after a day of them, one's nerves are really absolutely beat down. I can understand now why our infantry have to retreat sometimes; a sight which came as a shock to me at first, after being brought up in the belief that the English infantry cannot retreat.

[We are] in a dripping sodden wood, with the German trench in some places 40 yards ahead. . . . We had been worried by snipers all along and I had always been asking for leave to go out and have a try myself. Well, on Tuesday . . . they gave me leave. . . . Off I crawled through sodden clay and trenches going about a yard a minute. . . . Then I saw the Hun trench. . . . So I crawled on again very slowly to the parapet of the trench. . . .

Then the German behind me put his head up again. He was laughing and talking. I saw his teeth glistening against my foresight, and I pulled the trigger very slowly. He just grunted and crumpled up. . . .

[Something similar happened the next day.] I went back at a sort of galloping crawl to our lines and sent a message to the 10th that the Germans were moving up their way in some numbers. Half an hour afterward, they attacked the 10th and our right, in massed formation, advancing slowly to within 10 yards of the trenches. We simply mowed them down. It was rather horrible.

Source: Laurence Housman, ed., *War Letters of Fallen Englishmen* (London: E. P. Dutton, 1930), 119–20.

Source 20.1B
John Nash

Over the Top
1918

Over the Top, 1st Artists' Rifles at Marcoing, 30th December 1917, 1918 (oil on canvas), by John Northcote Nash (1893–1977)/Imperial War Museum, London, UK/© IWM (Art.IWM ART 1656)/Bridgeman Images

Source 20.1C
HUGO MUELLER

Letter from a German Soldier on the Western Front
1915

It has been extremely interesting to study the contents of the letter-cases of French killed and prisoners. The question frequently recurs, just as it does with us: "When will it all end?" To my astonishment I practically never found any expressions of hatred or abuse of Germany or German soldiers. On the other hand, many letters from relations revealed an absolute conviction of the justice of their cause and sometimes also of confidence in victory. In every letter, mother, fiancée, children, friends . . . spoke of a joyful return and speedy meeting — and now they are all lying dead and hardly even buried between the trenches, while over them bullets and shells sing their gruesome dirge. . . .

War hardens one's heart and blunts one's feelings, making a man indifferent to everything that formerly affected and moved him; but these qualities of hardness and indifference towards fate and death are necessary in the fierce battle to which trench warfare leads. Anybody who allowed himself to realize the whole tragedy of some of the daily occurrences in our life here would either lose his reason or be forced to bolt across the enemy's trench with his arms high in the air.

Source: Philipp Witkop, ed., *German Students' War Letters,* translated by Anne F. Wedd (London: Methuen, 1929), 278–79.

Source 20.1D
BEHARI LAL

Letter from a Soldier in the British Indian Army
1917

There is no likelihood of our getting rest during the winter. I am sure German prisoners could not be worse off in any way than we are. I had to go three nights without sleep, as I was on a motor lorry, and the lorry fellows, being Europeans, did not like to sleep with me, being an Indian. [The] cold was terrible, and it was raining hard; not being able to sleep on the ground in the open, I had to pass the whole night sitting on the outward lorry seats. I am sorry the hatred between Europeans and Indians is increasing instead of decreasing, and I am sure that the fault is not with the Indians. I am sorry to write this, which is not a hundredth part of what is in mind, but this increasing hatred and continued ill-treatment has compelled me to give you a hint.

Source: David Omussi, ed., *Indian Voices of the Great War* (New York: St. Martin's Press, 1999), 336–37.

Source 20.2
On the Home Front

The First World War is often described as an early example of "total war" in which the civilian population was both mobilized for the struggle and deeply affected by it. With so many men away from home, women were engaged with the war in any number of ways. Tens of thousands joined the military in support roles, particularly nursing, while in Russia several "women's battalions," all-female combat forces, were created in 1917, in part to stimulate war-weary men to continue the fight. This set of sources highlights some of the ways that women on the home front were involved in the Great War.

Source 20.2A, a British propaganda poster from 1915, and Source 20.2B, a popular British song, both speak to the moral expectation for women in wartime. Source 20.2C, from Germany, reflects a common experience of women during the war — work in military-related industries, while Source 20.2D reflects the food shortages afflicting German women owing to the Allied blockade of their country.

Questions to consider as you examine the sources:

- For what purposes did male authorities seek to mobilize women during the war?

- What is the message of the British propaganda poster in Source 20.2A to British men? And to British women?

- How is the relationship between social classes in wartime described or implied in Sources 20.2C and 20.2D?

Source 20.2A
Women of Britain Say – "Go!"
1915

Source 20.2B
Keep the Home Fires Burning
1915

They were summoned from the hillside, / They were called in from the glen,
And the country found them ready / At the stirring call for men.
Let no tears add to their hardships / As the soldiers pass along,
And although your heart is breaking, / Make it sing this cheery song:
Keep the Home Fires Burning, / While your hearts are yearning.

Though your lads are far away / They dream of home.
There's a silver lining / Through the dark clouds shining,
Turn the dark cloud inside out / Till the boys come home.

Source: Lena Guilbert Ford, "Keep the Home Fires Burning," music by Ivor Novello (London: Ascherberg Hopewood and the Crew, 1915).

Source 20.2C
Editha von Krell
Recollections of Four Months Working in a German Munitions Factory
1917

As the war went on, [the government] ordered two large munitions factories to be built right next to our town too. But very soon there was a shortage of male workers there. And so at the end of April 1917, all the town's women and girls were asked to come and work in these factories. . . . When we heard . . . that no one from the educated classes had yet volunteered, and that hundreds of workers were urgently required our decision was made. Together with two friends, my sister and I volunteered for duty immediately.

We began with an eight-hour shift from 3 in the afternoon to until 11 in the evening. . . . Initially we were all put in the sewing room where day after day we had to sew thousands of little bags which were then filled with barrel powder for the cartridges in another department. . . . We sewed without interruption — apart from a short coffee break and a half-hour supper break. . . . Our backs often hurt from this unaccustomed sitting. Our heads often ached terribly in the bad air, which you could almost have cut with a knife. . . . After a few weeks, at our own request, we were moved on to the "heavy work," where we had to put the howitzer shells together with the cases containing the powder and equip them with fuses. . . .

We were not allowed to air the rooms, even during our meal breaks. Doors and windows had to be kept shut because of the danger of explosions. But we prided ourselves on never slacking,

on always keeping up with the professional workers. Here too the harmonious relationships we
enjoyed with them was clear. For if ever this
completely unaccustomed work proved too much
for one of us [the educated women], one of the
workers would help out as a matter of course,
smiling, "Leave that to me, miss — it's far too hard
for you."

Even today we still like to think back to the
time when we were able to serve the Fatherland,
working with our hands at one with the people.

Source: *Deutsche Frauen, Deutsche Treue* [German Women, German
and Loyal], published in 1935. Reprinted in Joyce Marlow, ed.,
The Virago Book of Women and the Great War (London: Virago,
1998), 255–57. Used by permission.

Source 20.2D
Berlin Police Reports
1915

On the 16th of the month at 5:00 PM
thousands of women and children gathered
at the municipal market hall . . . to buy a few
pounds of potatoes. As the sale commenced, everyone stormed the market stands. The police, who
were trying to keep order, were simply overrun
and were powerless against the onslaught. A life-
threatening press at the stands ensued; each sought
to get past the next. . . . Women had their possessions ripped from them and children were tram-
pled on the ground as they pleaded for help. . . .
Women who got away from the crowds with
some ten pounds of potatoes each were bathed in
sweat and dropped to their knees from exhaustion before they could continue home. — Report
of Officer Rhein

I . . . came upon a crowd of several thousand men
and women who were howling loudly and pushing
the policemen aside. . . . [T]he crowd had already
stormed several buttershops because of the prices. . . .
Several large display windows were shattered, shop
doors destroyed, and entire stocks were simply
taken. . . . We cleared the street with fifteen mounted
officers. . . . Various objects such as flower pots were
thrown at us. — Report of Officer Krupphausen

Source: Brandenburgisches Landeshauptarchiv, Potsdam, Provinz
Brandenburg, Repositur 30, Berlin C, Titel 95, Polizeiprä-
sidium, Nrs. 15809, 15814, 15821, 15851. Contributed, translated, and introduced by Belinda Davis in *Lives and Voices:
Sources in European Women's History*, edited by Lisa DiCaprio
and Merry E. Wiesner (Boston: Wadsworth Publishing, 2000),
426–27. Used by permission.

Source 20.3
In the Aftermath of the Great War

Beyond the enormous political, social, and economic changes wrought
by World War I lay those transformations of consciousness, outlook, and
expectation that registered in the work of artists and writers as well as in the
sensibilities of individual people. This set of sources illustrates some of those
changes.

Among the many outcomes of the Great War was the presence in every
European country of disillusioned, maimed, and disfigured veterans, many

of them literally "men without faces." For some intellectuals and artists, they represented the fundamentally flawed civilization that had given rise to such carnage. Often neglected or overlooked, such men were reminders of a terrible past that others wanted to forget. The German artist Otto Dix (1891–1969), who served in his country's military forces throughout the war and was seriously wounded, portrayed this situation in a 1920 painting called *Prague Street*, here as Source 20.3A. Artistically, Dix worked in a style known as New Objectivity, which focused heavily on the horrendous outcomes of the war. Its practitioners deliberately included subject matter that was upsetting and even ugly, and they made little attempt to create unified images, preferring to present disconnected "particles of experience."

Source 20.3B derives from the most famous novel to emerge from the war. Written by the German war veteran Erich Maria Remarque, *All Quiet on the Western Front* describes the experience of a young German soldier and his classmates during the war. Published in 1929, it captured the sense of disillusionment and hopelessness that many returning veterans surely felt as they reentered civilian society. In Source 20.3C, a very different sense of self that derived from the war found expression in the recollections of an African veteran from Senegal, then a French colony in West Africa.

Questions to consider as you examine the source:

■ How does the painting in Source 20.3A describe the situation of the veterans? Notice the leaflet on the skateboard of the legless veteran at the bottom. It reads "Juden raus" (Jews out). What does this suggest about the political views of these men? What do the images in the store windows suggest?

■ How does Remarque in Source 20.3B describe the sensibility of those soldiers about to return to ordinary life? In describing the purpose of his book, Remarque wrote: "It will try simply to tell of a generation of men who, even though they may have escaped its shells, were destroyed by the war." How does the excerpt in Source 20.3B reflect that purpose?

■ How had the war changed the self-image of the Senegalese soldier in Source 20.3C? And how had it altered his standing within his own society and in relationship to Europeans? How and why was his experience so different from that described in Remarque's novel in Source 20.3B?

Source 20.3A
OTTO DIX

Prague Street
1920

Source 20.3B
ERICH MARIA REMARQUE

All Quiet on the Western Front
1929

Had we returned home in 1916, out of the suffering and the strength of our experiences we might have unleashed a storm. Now if we go back we will be weary, broken, burnt out, rootless, and without hope. We will not be able to find our way anymore.

And men will not understand us, for the generation that grew up before us, though it has passed these years with us, already had a home and a calling; now it will return to its old occupations, and the war will be forgotten; and the generation that has grown up after us will be strange to us and push us aside. We will be superfluous even to ourselves, we will grow older, a few will adapt themselves, some others will merely submit, and most will be bewildered; the years will pass by and in the end we shall fall into ruin.

But perhaps all this that I think is mere melancholy and dismay, which will fly away as the dust, when I stand once again beneath the poplars and listen to the rustling of their leaves. It cannot be that it has gone, the yearning that made our blood unquiet, the unknown, the perplexing, the oncoming things, the thousand faces of the future, the melodies from dreams and from books, the whispers and divinations of women; it cannot be that this has vanished in bombardment, in despair, in brothels. . . .

I stand up. I am very quiet. Let the months and years come, they can take nothing from me, they can take nothing more. I am so alone, and so without hope that I can confront them without fear.

Source: Erich Maria Remarque, *All Quiet on the Western Front*, translated by A. W. Wheen (New York: Ballantine Books, 1982), 293–95.

Source 20.3C
NAR DIOUF

A Senegalese Veteran's Oral Testimony
1919

I received many lasting things from the war. I demonstrated my dignity and courage, and [I] won the respect of the people and the [colonial] government. And whenever the people of the village had something to contest [with the French] — and they didn't dare do it [themselves] because they were afraid of them — I used to do it for them. And many times when people had problems with the government, I used to go with my decorations and arrange the situation for [them]. Because whenever the *Tubabs* [Europeans] saw your decorations, they knew that they [were dealing with] a very important person. . . . And I

gained this ability — of obtaining justice over a *Tubab* — from the war.

[For example], one day a *Tubab* came here [to the village] — . . . (he was a kind of doctor) — to make an examination of the people. So he came here, and there was a small boy who was blind. And [the boy] was walking, [but] he couldn't see, and he bumped into the *Tubab*. And the *Tubab* turned and pushed the boy [down]. And when I saw that, I came and said to the *Tubab*: "Why have you pushed this boy? [Can't] you see that he is blind?" And the *Tubab* said: "Oh, *pardon, pardon*. I did not know. I will never do it again, excuse me." [But] before the war, [no matter what they did], it would not have been possible to do that with a *Tubab*.

Source: Joe Lunn, *Memories of the Maelstrom: A Senegalese Oral History of the First World War* (Portsmouth, NH: Heinemann, 1999), 232. Used by permission of the author.

ESSAY QUESTIONS

Experiencing World War I

1. **Describing the war:** Based on these sources, how would you define the novel or distinctive features of World War I compared to earlier European conflicts?

2. **Considering war and progress:** How do you think the creators of these sources might have responded to the idea of "the perfectibility of humanity" described by Condorcet during the European Enlightenment of the eighteenth century? (See Source 15.3 in Thinking through Sources for Chapter 15.)

3. **Noticing what's missing:** What perspectives on the war are NOT reflected in these sources? Where might you look to find those perspectives?

CHAPTER 21

Experiencing Stalinism

For the Soviet Union, the formative period in establishing communism encompassed the years of Joseph Stalin's rule (1929–1953). Born in Georgia in 1878, rather than in Russia itself, the young Stalin grew up with a brutal and abusive father and trained for the priesthood as a young man, but slowly gravitated toward the emerging revolutionary movement of the time. He subsequently joined the Bolsheviks, led by Lenin, though he played only a modest role in the Russian Revolution of 1917. After Lenin's death in 1924, Stalin rose to the dominant position in the Communist Party amid a long and bitter struggle among the Bolsheviks. By 1929, he had consolidated his authority, and he exercised enormous personal power until his death in 1953.

To Stalin and the Soviet leadership, the 1930s was a time of "building socialism." Undertaking that gigantic task meant upheaval on an enormous scale, offering undreamed-of opportunities for some and disruption and trauma beyond imagination for others. The sources that follow allow us to see something of the Stalinist vision for the country as well as to gain some insight into the lives of ordinary people as they experienced what historians have come to call simply "Stalinism."

Source 21.1
Stalin on Stalinism

In January 1933, Stalin appeared before a group of high-ranking party officials to give a report on the achievements of the country's first five-year plan for overall development. The years encompassed by that plan, roughly 1928–1932, coincided with Stalin's rise to the position of supreme leader within the governing Communist Party of the Soviet Union.

Questions to consider as you examine the source:

■ What larger goals for the country underlay Stalin's report? Why did he believe these goals had to be achieved so rapidly?

■ To what indications of success did Stalin point? Which of these claims do you find most and least credible?

■ What do you think Stalin meant when he referred to the "world-wide historic significance" of the Soviet Union's achievement? Keep in mind what was happening in the capitalist world at the time.

JOSEPH STALIN

The Results of the First Five-Year Plan
1933

The fundamental task of the five-year plan was to convert the U.S.S.R. . . . into an industrial and powerful country, fully self-reliant and independent of the caprices of world capitalism, . . . to completely oust the capitalist elements, to widen the front of socialist forms of economy, and to create the economic basis for the abolition of classes in the U.S.S.R., for the building of a socialist society. . . .

Let us pass now to the results of the fulfillment of the five-year plan. . . .

We did not have an iron and steel industry, the basis for the industrialization of the country. Now we have one.

[*Stalin follows with a long list of new industries developed during the first five-year plan: tractors, automobiles, machine tools, chemicals, agricultural machinery, electric power, oil and coal, metals.*]

And we have not only created these new great industries, but have created them on a scale and in dimensions that eclipse . . . European industry.

And as a result of all this the capitalist elements have been completely and irrevocably ousted from industry, and socialist industry has become the sole form of industry in the U.S.S.R. . . .

Finally, as a result of all this the Soviet Union has been converted from a weak country, unprepared for defense, into a country mighty in defense . . . , a country capable of producing on a mass scale all modern means of defense and of equipping its army with them in the event of an attack from abroad.

We are told: This is all very well; many new factories have been built, and the foundations for industrialization have been laid; but it would have been far better . . . to produce more cotton fabrics, shoes, clothing, and other goods for mass consumption. . . . Then we would now have more cotton fabrics, shoes, and clothing. But we would not have a tractor industry or an automobile industry; we would not have anything like a big iron and steel industry; we would not have metal for the manufacture of machinery — and we would remain unarmed while encircled by capitalist countries armed with modern technique. . . .

It was necessary to urge forward a country which was a hundred years behindhand and which was faced with mortal danger because of its backwardness. . . .

The five-year plan in the sphere of agriculture was a five-year plan of collectivization. . . . [I]t was necessary in addition to industrialization, to pass from small, individual peasant farming to . . . large collective farms, equipped with all the modern implements of highly developed agriculture, and to cover unoccupied land with model state farms. . . .

The Party has succeeded in routing the kulaks [relatively well-off peasants] as a class, although they have not yet been dealt the final blow; the laboring peasants have been emancipated from kulak bondage and exploitation, and the Soviet regime has been given a firm economic basis in the countryside, the basis of collective farming.

In our country, the workers have long forgotten unemployment. . . . Look at the capitalist countries: what horrors result there from unemployment! There are now no less than 30–40 million unemployed in those countries. . . .

The same thing must be said of the peasants. . . . It has brought them into the collective farms and placed them in a secure position. It has thus eliminated the possibility of the differentiation of the peasantry into exploiters — kulaks — and exploited — poor peasants — and abolished destitution in the countryside. . . . Now the peasant is in a position of security, a member of a collective farm which has at its disposal tractors, agricultural machinery, seed funds, reserve funds. . . .

[W]e have achieved such important successes as to evoke admiration among the working class all over the world; we have achieved a victory that is truly of world-wide historic significance.

Source: Joseph Stalin, "The Results of the First Five-Year Plan," *Pravda*, January 10, 1933.

Source 21.2
Collectivization: A Stalinist Vision

For Russian peasants, and those of other nationalities as well, the chief experience of Stalinism was collectivization — the enforced bringing together of many small-scale family farms into much larger collective farms called *kolhozy*. Thus private ownership of land was largely ended, even as the somewhat better-off peasants, known as *kulaks,* were dispossessed, deported, and sometimes killed. Collectivization was undertaken from the outside, largely by urban Communist Party activists fired with enthusiasm for socialism and modernity and eager to overcome what they saw as the backwardness and "darkness" of the countryside. One such young woman wrote to a friend: "I am off in villages with a group of other brigadiers organizing kolhozy. It is a tremendous job, but we are making amazing progress . . . , draw[ing] the stubborn peasant into collectivization. . . . [O]ur muzhik [peasant] is yielding to persuasion. He is joining the kolhozy, and I am confident that in time not a peasant will remain on his own land. We shall yet smash the last vestiges of capitalism and forever rid ourselves of exploitation. . . . The very air here is afire with a new spirit and a new energy."[1]

In seeking to persuade reluctant peasants to join the new collective farms, such enthusiastic young party workers presented an attractive picture of the future. "Just look at yourself," declared Kostia Lutkov, one of the organizers, to an audience of young villagers, "your coat is all torn; you're wearing bast shoes [made from tree bark]; and your pants are made from sackcloth. Now in the collective farm, you could make some money, receive your grain ration, and even buy cologne for your evening get-togethers. . . . Just think about it. . . . All the land will be collectivized, so the kolkhoz will have plenty of it; all the horses will be in the same stable in the large collective farm yard; and all the machines — harvesting, sowing, and threshing — will stand next to each

other in the same collective farm yard. With all that land and all those horses and machines — if you work hard, you will be well-fed and well dressed."[2]

That hopeful and idealized vision of what socialist agriculture could become was expressed in Source 21.2, a Soviet poster from 1930, titled *The Day of Harvest and Collectivization*.

Questions to consider as you examine the sources:

- How would you describe that vision? How does it compare with the past represented by the two small circles with an "X"? What message about gender does the poster convey?

- In what ways does the poster reflect Stalin's vision for the country as expressed in Source 21.1?

- The sign at the center right of the image reads "Collective Farm: Godless/Atheist." What does this suggest about the official outlook of the Stalinist regime?

The Day of Harvest and Collectivization
1930

Source 21.3
Living through Collectivization

The reality of collectivization was often quite different from the perspective of those undergoing the process, as the following set of sources illustrates. Source 21.3A details one of the most painful aspects of collectivization — the expulsion of *kulaks,* or rich peasants, believed by communist authorities to bear the germs of rural capitalism and to be unalterably opposed to socialism. Many of those who remained on the collective farms deeply resented the regimentation, often branding their role as slavery or even a "second serfdom." Furthermore the government's persistent demand for more grain from the collective farms, which was needed to support the industrialization drive, contributed to a terrible famine in the early 1930s that led to millions of deaths. Source 21.3B comes from a report by a Communist Party official on the desperate conditions in the collective farms near Novosibirsk in Siberia during that time. Even after the famine had passed, life on the collective farms remained intolerable for many, as reflected in Source 21.3C, a letter written by a peasant to a Russian official in 1937.

Questions to consider as you examine the sources:

- In what ways did the realities of collectivization contradict Stalin's high hopes for the movement?

- Construct an imaginary debate between an activist supporter of the collective farms and a peasant opponent.

- Why were Stalin and the Communist Party so insistent on destroying the kulaks?

Source 21.3A
ANNA AKIMOVNA DUBOVA

"Branded Kulaks and Dispossessed"
1928–1929

[E]veryone was opposed to joining the kolkhoz, but people were forced to join. If someone resisted, he was punished and everything was taken from him — his land, his animals, everything he had. People were literally herded onto the kolkhoz.... We were branded kulaks and dispossessed. They took away our vote because we had this shop and engaged in trade. Then in 1929 forced requisitioning of grain began and they started imposing taxes in kind, procurement quotas, and who did they impose them on? On *lishentsy* ["deprived ones," peasants accused of being kulaks], of course.... So my father was put in prison for not meeting [quotas]....

They wanted to deport us. But then I guess some chairman must have taken pity on us.... Now the poor peasants, or *bednota,* immediately went after our possessions. They were filled

with such hatred. "Why should they have lived so well?" But others were deported in our place [*to meet government quotas for dispossession of kulaks in various regions*]. . . . We were told that we could settle wherever we wanted, to get going, and everything was taken from us, everything. I remember so well how Mama sat and cried when they took away the cow. Then they took away the horse. . . . They took down the mirror, took away the bed . . . and then said "get out of here." . . .

No one would take us in any longer. Everybody was afraid that they would be accused of harboring kulaks, that people would say, "Aha, so you're sympathetic to kulaks. That's it for you; you'll be deported too." I remember how Mother went to her brother, to her own father and mother, to the very spot where she had been married, and even they couldn't keep her.

Source: *A Revolution of Their Own: Voices of Women in Soviet History* by Engel, Barbara Alpern; Posadskaya-Vanderbeck, Anastasia; Hoisington, Sona Stephan, 1941. Reproduced with permission of WESTVIEW PRESS in the format Republish in a book via Copyright Clearance Center.

Source 21.3B
Letter from Feigin to Ordzhonikidze
April 9, 1932

I was in various kolkhozes . . . , but everywhere there was only one sight — that of a huge shortage of seed, famine, and extreme emaciation of livestock.

In the kolkhozes which I observed I attempted to learn how much the livestock had diminished in comparison with the years 1927–28. It turns out that kolkhoz Ziuzia has 507 milch cows at present while there were 2000 in 1928. . . .

The situation of the kolkhoz livestock farms is a bad one, primarily because of lack of feed. Milk production has reached extremely low levels of 1, 2 or 3 liters per day instead of the 5–7 liters normal for this region in a high-yield year. . . . The main issue is the fact that almost all of the kolkhozniks' [residents of the collective farms] livestock is contracted [by the state] and removed. . . . In addition, when this livestock is contracted, the kolkhoznik and individual farmers slaughter off the rest.

The second item concerns the sowing campaign. The situation is such that there is not enough seed in the kolkhozes. There is no way that we will be able to fulfill the plan for grain production. . . . Besides this, horses are quite emaciated, a significant number of them have already died, and in addition, the people do not have provisions.

Third issue — the peasant's attitude. Their attitude is utterly bad in light of the famine and the fact that they are losing their last cows through contracting — as a result the kolkhoznik has neither bread nor milk. I saw all this with my own eyes and am not exaggerating. People are starving, living on food substitutes, they grow weaker, and naturally, under such circumstances, their mood is hostile.

Source: Letter from Feigin to Ordzhonikidze, April 9, 1932, "Revelations from the Russian Archives: Collectivization of Livestock," Library of Congress, http://www.loc.gov/exhibits /archives/aa2feign.html.

Source 21.3C
Leaving the Collective Farms
1937

I read . . . about the achievements of the collective farms, but that's all window-dressing. If you look inside the collective farms, then it will surely be the opposite. . . . What really shows how things are is the way the kolkhozniks are leaving the collective farms. . . . If you count the old population that used to be in the [villages], only 50 percent is still there. That fact demonstrates that people are unwilling to live in kolkhoz. . . .

But what explains the kolkhozniks' departure from the collective farms? I think it is that the kolkhozy and the kolkhozniks are insulted by the government. And this is why: If you compare workers in factories, they live better than kolkhozniks. If you want to prove that — there are kolkhozniks who left the collective farms two years ago and got jobs at factories and enterprises,

and they write that now it has become better to live at the mills and factories than in the kolkhozy. There you know how much you earn every day, they write; you can make 15 rubles and more at the factory; you can buy cloth and other goods too, as much as you want; and they write "I live much better here than in the kolkhoz."

But just let the kolkhoznik try to buy something where *he* lives — you can't buy cloth here and the kolkhoznik goes around badly dressed. . . . Now what we have is a pecking order in real life in which the kolkhozniks have missed the boat and you can't get any lower than the village.

Source: Quoted in Sheila Fitzpatrick, *Stalin's Peasants* (Oxford: Oxford University Press, 1994), 102.

Source 21.4
Industrialization and Religion: A Stalinist Vision

Another core feature of the Stalinist era was rapid state-controlled industrialization. In Stalin's thinking, the urgency of the task was reinforced by Russia's history of military defeats at the hands of more powerful enemies from the Mongols to the British, French, and Germans. "To slacken the tempo would mean falling behind," Stalin declared. "And those who fall behind get beaten. . . . Do you want our socialist fatherland to be beaten and to lose its independence? If you do not want this, you must put an end to its backwardness in the shortest possible time and develop genuine Bolshevik tempo in building up its socialist system of economy. . . . We are fifty to a hundred years behind the advanced countries. We must make good this distance in ten years. Either we shall do it or we shall go under."[3]

But industrialization would not only provide for the defense of the country but also lay the foundation for an enormous social and cultural transformation appropriate for a distinctly socialist society. An important element of Soviet cultural policy lay in the struggle against both religion and alcoholism. The poster in Source 21.4 illustrates the relationship among the industrial drive, the Communist Party's hostility to organized religion, and its efforts to curb alcoholism. It is titled *Religion Is the Enemy of Industrialization* and derives from a Soviet temperance organization called The Morning After.

Questions to consider as you examine the sources:

- Why might communist leaders consider religion and alcoholism as enemies of industrialization? What elements of the poster convey this message?

- How are the religious figures on the left side portrayed? Who might the string-pulling figures on a cloud represent?

- How is the communist worker on the right contrasted with the religiously influenced worker on the left? Notice that the communist worker is reading a copy of a magazine called *The Godless*.

Religion Is the Enemy of Industrialization

RIA Novosti/akg-images

Source 21.5
Living through Stalinist Industrialization: Personal Accounts of Soviet Industrialization, 1930s

The brief excerpts in Source 21.5 present a range of voices from those who experienced their country's drive to industrial development during the 1930s. Some celebrated the new possibilities, while others lamented the disappointments and injustices of Stalinist industrialization. These sources come from letters written to newspapers or to high government officials, from private letters and diaries, or from reports filed by party officials based on what they had heard in the factories.

Questions to consider as you examine the sources:

■ In what respects did Soviet workers benefit from Stalinist industrialization?

■ What criticisms were voiced in these extracts? Do they represent fundamental opposition to the idea of socialism or disappointments in how it was implemented?

■ Through its control of education and the media, the Stalinist regime sought to instill a single view of the world in its citizens. Based on these selections, to what extent had they succeeded or failed?

Source 21.5A
Letter in a Newspaper from a Tatar Electrician

I am a Tatar [a Turko/Mongol ethnic group]. . . . [I]n old tsarist Russia, we weren't even considered people. We couldn't even dream about education, or getting a job in a state enterprise. And now I'm a citizen of the USSR. Like all citizens, I have the right to a job, to education, to leisure. I can elect and be elected to the soviet [legislative council]. Is this not an indication of the supreme achievements of our country? . . .

Two years ago I worked as the chairman of a village soviet in the Tatar republic. I was the first person there to enter the kolhoz and then I led the collectivization campaign. Collective farming is flourishing with each year in the Tatar republic.

In 1931 I came to Magnitogorsk [a major industrial site]. From a common laborer I have turned into a skilled worker. I was elected a member of the city soviet. As a deputy, every day I receive workers who have questions or need help. I listen to each one like to my own brother, and try to do what is necessary to make each one satisfied.

I live in a country where one feels like living and learning. And if the enemy should attack this country, I will sacrifice my life in order to destroy the enemy and save my country.

Source 21.5B
Newspaper Commentary by an Engineer
1938

Soon it will be seven years that I'm working in Magnitogorsk. With my own eyes I've seen the pulsating, creative life of the builders of the Magnitogorsk giant. I myself have taken an active part in this construction with great enthusiasm. Our joy was great when we obtained the first Magnitogorsk steel from the wonderful open-hearth ovens. At the time there was no greater happiness for me than working in the open-hearth shop. . . . Here I enriched my theoretical knowledge and picked up practical habits . . . of work. Here as well I grew politically, acquired good experience in public-political work. I came to Magnitogorsk non-party. The party organization . . . accepted me into a group of sympathizers. Not long ago I entered the ranks of the Leninist-Stalinist [communist] party. . . . I love my hometown Magnitka with all my heart. I consider my work at the Magnitogorsk factory to be a special honor and high trust shown to me, a Soviet engineer, by the country.

Source 21.5C
Letter to a Soviet Official from a Worker
1938

In fact, there's been twenty years of our [Soviet] power. Fifteen to sixteen of these have been peaceful construction. . . . The people struggled with zeal, overcame difficulties. Socialism has been built in the main. As we embark on the third five-year plan we shout at meetings, congresses, and in newspapers "Hurray, we have reached a happy, joyful life!" However, incidentally, if one is to be honest, those shouts are mechanical, made from habit, pumped by social organizations. The ordinary person makes such speeches like a street newspaper-seller. In fact, in his heart, when he comes home, this bawler, eulogist, will agree with his family, his wife who reproaches him that today she has been torturing herself in queues and did not get anything — there are no suits, no coats, no meat, no butter.

Source 21.5D
Letter from a Student to His Teacher

I worked at a factory for five years. Now I'll have to leave my studies at the institute. Who will study? Very talented Lomonosovs [brilliant students] and the sons of Soviet rulers, since they have the highest posts and are the best paid. In this way education will be available only to the highest strata (a sort of nobility), while for the lowest strata, the laboring people, the doors will be closed.

Source 21.5E
Two Comments from Factory Workers Found in Soviet Archives
1930s

What is there to say about the successes of Soviet power? It's lies. The newspapers cover up the real state of things. I am a worker, wear torn clothes, my four children go to school half-starving, in rags. I, an honest worker, am a visible example of what Soviet power has given the workers in the last twenty years.

How can we liquidate classes, if new classes have developed here, with the only difference being that they are not called classes? Now there are the same parasites who live at the expense of others. The worker produces and at the same time works for many people who live off him. From the example of our factory it is clear that there is a huge apparat of factory administrators, where idlers sit. There are many administrative workers who travel about in cars and get three to four times more than the worker. These people live in the best conditions and live at the expense of the labor of the working class.

Source 21.5F
Entry from a Worker's Diary
1936

[T]he portraits of party leaders are now displayed the same way icons used to be: a round portrait framed and attached to a pole. Very convenient, hoist it onto your shoulder and you're on your way. And all these preparations are just like what people used to do before church holidays. . . . They had their own activists then, we have ours now. Different paths, the same old folderol.

Source 21.5G
Comment from an Anonymous Communist in Soviet Archives
1938

Do you not think that comrade Stalin's name has begun to be very much abused? . . . Everything is Stalin, Stalin, Stalin. You only have to listen to a radio program about our achievements, and every fifth or tenth word will be the name of comrade Stalin. In the end this sacred and beloved name — Stalin — may make so much noise in people's heads that it is very possible that it will have the opposite effect.

Sources: Selections A and B: *Magnetic Mountain: Stalinism as a Civilization* by Stephen Kotkin, © 1996 by the Regents of the University of California. Published by the University of California Press. Used by permission of the University of California Press; selections C through G: Sarah Davies, *Popular Opinion in Stalin's Russia*. Copyright © 1997 Sarah Davies. Reprinted with the permission of Cambridge University Press.

Source 21.6
Living through the Stalinist Terror

More than anything else, it was the Terror — sometimes called the Great Purges — that came to define Stalinism as a distinctive phenomenon in the history of Soviet communism. Millions of people were caught up in this vast process of identifying and eliminating so-called "enemies of the people," many of them loyal communist citizens. Source 21.6A provides an excerpt from the memoirs of Irina Kakhovskaya, an ardent revolutionary, though not a party member, who was arrested in 1937 and spent seventeen years either in prison or in a labor camp. Here she describes her arrest and interrogation. Source 21.6B comes from the experience of Eugenia Ginsberg, a woman who survived many years in perhaps the most notorious of the gulag camps — Kolyma in the frigid northeastern corner of the Soviet Union. In this selection, Ginsberg recounts an ordinary day in the camps. Beyond those arrested, killed, or imprisoned during Stalin's terror were those left behind, fearful of their own arrest, anxiously awaiting news of their missing loved ones, or endlessly waiting in line to seek information about them or to send parcels to them. In Source 21.6C, Inna Shikheeva-Gaister recounts her efforts to send packages to her imprisoned mother.

Questions to consider as you examine the sources:

■ In what different ways did people experience the Stalinist Terror? What do you think motivated each of these women who wrote about it?

■ What might you infer from these selections about the purposes of the Terror, the means by which it was implemented, and its likely outcomes, whether intended or not?

■ Many innocent people who were arrested believed that others were guilty as charged, while in their own case a mistake had been made. How might you account for this widespread response to the Terror?

Source 21.6A
Irina Kakhovskaya

Arrest and Interrogation
1937

Early on the morning of February 8, 1937, a large group of men appeared at the door of our quiet apartment in Ufa. We were shown a search warrant and warrants for our arrest. The search was carried out in violent, pogrom-like fashion and lasted all day. Books went pouring down from the shelves; letters and papers, out of boxes. They tapped the walls and, when they encountered hollow spots, removed the bricks. Everything was covered with dust and pieces of brick. . . .

At the prison everything was aimed at breaking prisoners' spirits immediately, intimidating and stupefying them, making them feel that they were no longer human, but "enemies of the people," against whom everything was permitted. All elementary human needs were disregarded (light, air, food, rest, medical care, warmth, toilet facilities). . . .

In the tiny, damp, cold, half-lit cell were a bunk and a half bunk. The bunk was for the prisoner under investigation and on the half bunk, their legs drawn up, the voluntary victims, the informers from among the common criminals, huddled together. Their duty was never to let their neighbor out of their sight, never to let the politicals communicate with one another . . . and above all to prevent the politicals from committing suicide. . . . The air was fouled by the huge wooden latrine bucket. . . .

The interrogation began on the very first night. . . . Using threats, endearments, promises and enigmatic hints, they tried to confuse, wear down, frighten, and break the will of each individual, who was kept totally isolated from his or her comrades. . . . Later stools were removed and the victim had to simply stand for hours on end. . . .

At first it seemed that the whole thing was a tremendous and terrible misunderstanding, that it was our duty to clear it up. . . . But it soon became apparent that what was involved was deliberate ill will and the most cynical possible approach to the truth. . . .

In the interrogation sessions, I now had several investigators in a row, and the "conveyor belt" questioning would go on for six days and nights on end. . . . Exhaustion reached the ultimate limit. The brain, inadequately supplied with blood, began to misfunction. . . . "Sign! We won't bother you anymore. We'll give you a quiet cell and a pillow and you can sleep. . . ." That was how the investigator would try to bribe a person who was completely debilitated and stupefied from lack of sleep.

Each of us fought alone to keep an honest name and save the honor of our friends, although it would have been far easier to die than to endure this hell month after month. Nevertheless the accused remained strong in spirit and, apart from the unfortunate Mayorov, not one real revolutionary did they manage to break.

Source: Irina Kakhovskaya, "Our Fate," From *An End to Silence: Uncensored Opinion in the Soviet Union,* edited by Stephen Cohen, translated by George Saunders. Copyright © 1982 by W. W. Norton & Company, Inc. Used by permission of W. W. Norton & Company, Inc. This selection may not be reproduced, stored in a retrieval system, or transmitted in any form or by any means without the prior written permission of the publisher.

Source 21.6B
Eugenia Ginsberg

A Day in Kolyma
1939

The work to which I was assigned . . . went by the imposing name of "land improvement." We set out before dawn and marched in ranks of five for about three miles, to the accompaniment of shouts from the guards and bad language from the common criminals who were included in our party as a punishment for some misdeed or other. In time we reached a bleak, open field where our leader, another common criminal called Senka — a disgusting type who preyed on the other prisoners and made no bones about offering a pair of warm breeches in return for an hour's "fun and games" — handed out picks and iron spades with which we attacked the frozen soil of Kolyma until one in the afternoon. I cannot remember, and perhaps I never knew, the rational purpose this "improvement" was supposed to serve. I only remember the ferocious wind, the forty-degree frost, the appalling weight of the pick, and the wild, irregular thumping of one's heart. At one o'clock we were marched back for dinner. More stumbling in and out of snowdrifts, more shouts and threats from the guards whenever we fell out of line. Back in the camp we received our longed-for piece of bread and soup and were allowed half an hour in which to huddle around the stove in the hope of absorbing enough warmth to last us halfway back to the field. After we had toiled again with our picks and spades till late in the evening, Senka would come and survey what we had done and abuse us for not doing more. How could the assignment ever be completed if we spoiled women fulfilled only thirty percent of the norm? . . . Finally a night's rest, full of nightmares, and the dreaded banging of a hammer on an iron rail which was the signal for a new day to begin.

Source: Eugenia Semyonovna Ginzburg, *Journey into the Whirlwind* (New York: Harcourt, Brace Jovanovich, 1967), 366–67.

Source 21.6C
INNA SHIKHEEVA-GAISTER

Sending a Parcel
1938

I started sending parcels to my mother. . . . I was thrilled if I managed to do it once a month. At first they accepted parcels in Moscow, but that soon ended because on those days [when parcels were accepted] the post office lines would be longer than those in the grocery stores. After that we had to go to Aleksandrov or Mozhaisk — that is about two hundred kilometers outside Moscow. . . .

They would only accept a limited number of parcels, so if you got there late, they might close the window before your turn came. . . . When the train arrived in Mozhaisk, there would be a terrible stampede. . . . Everyone would be running like crazy, pushing and shoving, trying to get ahead. In the beginning I was frightened, but then I got used to it.

The parcel had to weigh exactly eight kilos — no more no less. Imagine standing in that line and then having your parcel rejected because of an extra two hundred grams. . . . If it was too heavy, you had to open your box and take something out. In the meantime you might miss your turn; then you would try to push your way back through to the window, with the people in line acting like wild animals, growling and pouncing on one another. . . . If you finally had it accepted, you would walk back to the station in a state of utter bliss — as if you had just come out of a bathhouse after a good steam.

Source: Inna Shikheeva-Gaister, "A Family Chronicle," in *In the Shadow of Revolution: Life Stories of Russian Women, from 1917 to the Second World War*, edited by Sheila Fitzpatrick and Yuri Slezkine (Princeton, NJ: Princeton University Press, 2000), 386–87.

ESSAY QUESTIONS

Experiencing Stalinism

1. **Defending Stalinism:** Develop an argument that the fundamental goals of Stalinism (building socialism) were largely achieved during the 1930s.

2. **Criticizing Stalinism:** Develop an argument that socialist ideals and values were essentially betrayed or perverted by the developments of the Stalin era.

3. **Assessing change:** In what ways did the Stalin era represent a revolutionary transformation of Soviet society? In what ways did it continue older patterns of Russian history?

4. **Considering moral judgments:** Why do you think that historians have found it so difficult to write about the Stalin era without passing judgment on it? Does this represent a serious problem for scholars? Should students of the past seek to avoid moral judgments or are they an inevitable, perhaps even useful, part of the historian's craft?

Notes

1. Maurice Hindus, *Red Bread: Collectivization in a Russian Village* (Bloomington: Indiana University Press, 1988), 1.

2. Sheila Fitzpatrick and Yuri Slezkine, eds., *In the Shadow of Revolution: Life Stories of Russian Women, from 1917 to the Second World War* (Princeton, NJ: Princeton University Press, 2000), 237.

3. J. V. Stalin, *Problems of Leninism* (Moscow: Foreign Languages Publishing House, 1953), 454–58. Available at http://academic.shu.edu/russianhistory/index.php/Stalin_on_Rapid_Industrialization.

CHAPTER 22

THINKING THROUGH SOURCES

Articulating Independence

For millions of people in Africa, Asia, Oceania, and the Caribbean, the achievement of political independence from colonial rule and foreign domination marked a singular moment in their personal lives and in their collective histories. That achievement had taken shape in many different ways, with variation in the duration and intensity of the struggle, in the tactics of the independence movements, and in the ideologies that they espoused. Here, however, we focus less on the process by which independence was acquired than on the various meanings ascribed to it. Everywhere the moment of independence represented a surprising triumph against great odds and an awakening to the possibility of building new lives and new societies. The sources that follow reflect the hopes, aspirations, and warnings of that remarkable moment. Many of the most ambitious goals subsequently went unfulfilled or were betrayed, fueling immense disappointment. Nonetheless it is worth reflecting on the varied meanings associated with the coming of independence, for in human affairs, almost always, our reach exceeds our grasp.

Source 22.1
Declaring Vietnam's Independence

Just a few weeks after the end of World War II in Asia, Ho Chi Minh, the nationalist and communist leader of his country's independence movement, declared Vietnam free of both five years of Japanese control and over sixty years of French colonial rule. The date was September 2, 1945, and the place was Hanoi, the colonial capital of French Indochina. Over thirty more years of struggle lay ahead, first against French efforts to reestablish colonial rule over Vietnam and then against American military intervention in the country. But the Declaration of 1945 spoke to the meaning of that struggle, largely by referring to the colonial past, to the legacy of the Atlantic revolutions, and to the proclaimed values of the victors in World War II.

Questions to consider as you examine the source:

■ In what ways does the Declaration seek to legitimate Vietnam's independence?

■ What critique of colonial rule is contained in the Declaration?

■ How does the Declaration seek to situate Vietnam's independence struggle both historically and in terms of the global politics of 1945?

Declaration of Independence of the Democratic Republic of Vietnam
September 2, 1945

"All men are created equal. They are endowed by their Creator with certain inalienable rights, among them are Life, Liberty, and the pursuit of Happiness." This immortal statement was made in the Declaration of Independence of the United States of America in 1776. In a broader sense, this means: All the peoples on the earth are equal from birth, all the peoples have a right to live, to be happy and free.

The Declaration of the French Revolution made in 1791 on the Rights of Man and the Citizen also states: "All men are born free and with equal rights, and must always remain free and have equal rights." Those are undeniable truths.

Nevertheless, for more than eighty years, the French imperialists, abusing the standard of Liberty, Equality, and Fraternity, have violated our Fatherland and oppressed our fellow-citizens. They have acted contrary to the ideals of humanity and justice.

In the field of politics, they have deprived our people of every democratic liberty.

They have enforced inhuman laws; they have set up three distinct political regimes in the North, the Center and the South of Vietnam in order to wreck our national unity and prevent our people from being united.

They have built more prisons than schools. They have mercilessly slain our patriots; they have drowned our uprisings in rivers of blood.

To weaken our race they have forced us to use opium and alcohol.

In the field of economics, they have fleeced us to the backbone, impoverished our people, and devastated our land.

They have robbed us of our rice fields, our mines, our forests, and our raw materials. They have monopolized the issuing of bank-notes and the export trade.

They have invented numerous unjustifiable taxes and reduced our people, especially our peasantry, to a state of extreme poverty.

They have hampered the prospering of our national bourgeoisie; they have mercilessly exploited our workers.

In the autumn of 1940, when the Japanese Fascists violated Indochina's territory to establish new bases in their fight against the Allies, the French imperialists went down on their bended knees and handed over our country to them.

Thus, from that date, our people were subjected to the double yoke of the French and the Japanese. Their sufferings and miseries increased. . . . Notwithstanding all this, our fellow-citizens have always manifested toward the French a tolerant and humane attitude. . . . The Vietminh League helped many Frenchmen to cross the frontier, rescued some of them from Japanese jails, and protected French lives and property. From the autumn of 1940, our country had in fact ceased to be a French colony and had become a Japanese possession.

After the Japanese had surrendered to the Allies, our whole people rose to regain our national sovereignty and to found the Democratic Republic of Vietnam. The truth is that we have wrested our independence from the Japanese and not from the French.

Our people have broken the chains which for nearly a century have fettered them and have won independence for the Fatherland. Our people at the same time have overthrown the monarchic regime that has reigned supreme for dozens of centuries. In its place has been established the present Democratic Republic.

For these reasons, we, members of the Provisional Government, representing the whole Vietnamese people, declare that from now on we break off all relations of a colonial character with France; we repeal all the international obligations that France has so far subscribed to on behalf of Vietnam and we abolish all the special rights the French have unlawfully acquired in our Fatherland.

The whole Vietnamese people, animated by a common purpose, are determined to fight to the bitter end against any attempt by the French colonialists to reconquer their country.

We are convinced that the Allied nations which at Tehran [where Roosevelt, Churchill, and Stalin met] and San Francisco [where the United Nations was established] have acknowledged the principles of self-determination and equality of nations, will not refuse to acknowledge the independence of Vietnam.

A people who have courageously opposed French domination for more than eight years, a people who have fought side by side with the Allies against the Fascists during these last years, such a people must be free and independent.

For these reasons, we, members of the Provisional Government of the Democratic Republic of Vietnam, solemnly declare to the world that Vietnam has the right to be a free and independent country — and in fact is so already. The entire Vietnamese people are determined to mobilize all their physical and mental strength, to sacrifice their lives and property in order to safeguard their independence and liberty.

Source: Ho Chi Minh, *Selected Works*, vol. 3 (Hanoi: Foreign Languages Publishing House, 1960–62), 17–21.

Source 22.2
Vietnam's Independence: Fifty Years Later

In 1995, Vietnam marked the fiftieth anniversary of its earlier Declaration of Independence, an event celebrated by this poster. Pictured on the right side of the poster is Ho Chi Minh, the principal author of the earlier Declaration, who had died in 1969. The caption refers to a "National Day" commemoration for what had become a "unified and socialist" country.

Questions to consider as you examine the source:

■ What does the poster suggest have been the country's major achievements since independence?

■ What is the significance of the tanks and soldiers shown in red at the upper left of the poster?

■ Does the poster emphasize Vietnam's nationalist or its communist achievements?

Fiftieth Anniversary of Vietnamese Independence

Color lithograph by Phuong Van Luong/Private Collection/Bridgeman Images

Source 22.3
India's "Tryst with Destiny"

Just two years after Ho Chi Minh announced Vietnam's independence, Jawaharlal Nehru did the same for India, shortly before midnight on August 14, 1947. Hovering over this joyful event was the tragedy of the bloody partition between India and Pakistan and the absence at the celebration of India's great nationalist leader, Gandhi, who was in Calcutta, praying, fasting, and seeking to stem the violence between Muslims and Hindus.

Questions to consider as you examine the source:

■ How does Nehru's speech compare with Ho Chi Minh's Declaration?

■ What kind of India does Nehru foresee emerging from the struggle for independence? How does his vision compare with that of Gandhi? (See Source 18.5 in the Thinking through Sources feature for Chapter 18.)

■ What aspects of Indian society posed a challenge for the India of Nehru's hopes?

JAWAHARLAL NEHRU

Independence Day Speech
August 14, 1947

Long years ago we made a tryst with destiny, and now the time comes when we shall redeem our pledge, not wholly or in full measure, but very substantially. At the stroke of the midnight hour, when the world sleeps, India will awake to life and freedom. A moment comes, which comes but rarely in history, when we step out from the old to the new, when an age ends, and when the soul of a nation, long suppressed, finds utterance. It is fitting that at this solemn moment we take the pledge of dedication to the service of India and her people and to the still larger cause of humanity. . . .

Before the birth of freedom we have endured all the pains of labour and our hearts are heavy with the memory of this sorrow. Some of those pains continue even now. Nevertheless, the past is over and it is the future that beckons to us now.

That future is not one of ease or resting but of incessant striving so that we may fulfil the pledges we have so often taken and the one we shall take today. The service of India means the service of the millions who suffer. It means the ending of poverty and ignorance and disease and inequality of opportunity. The ambition of the greatest man of our generation [Gandhi] has been to wipe every tear from every eye. That may be beyond us, but as long as there are tears and suffering, so long our work will not be over.

And so we have to labour and to work, and work hard, to give reality to our dreams. Those dreams are for India, but they are also for the world, for all the nations and peoples are too closely knit together today for any one of them to imagine that it can live apart. Peace has been said to be indivisible; so is freedom, so is prosperity now, and so also is disaster in this One World that can no longer be split into isolated fragments.

To the people of India, whose representatives we are, we make an appeal to join us with faith and confidence in this great adventure. This is no time for petty and destructive criticism, no time for ill-will or blaming others. We have to build the noble mansion of free India where all her children may dwell.

The appointed day has come — the day appointed by destiny — and India stands forth again, after long slumber and struggle, awake, vital, free and independent. The past clings on to us still in some measure and we have to do much before we redeem the pledges we have so often taken. Yet the turning-point is past, and history begins anew for us, the history which we shall live and act and others will write about.

It is a fateful moment for us in India, for all Asia and for the world. A new star rises, the star of freedom in the East, a new hope comes into being, a vision long cherished materializes. . . . On this day our first thoughts go to the architect of this freedom, the Father of our Nation [Gandhi], who, embodying the old spirit of India, held aloft the torch of freedom and lighted up the darkness that surrounded us. We have often been unworthy followers of his and have strayed from his message, but not only we but succeeding generations will remember this message and bear the imprint in their hearts of this great son of India, magnificent in his faith and strength and courage and humility. . . .

The future beckons to us. Whither do we go and what shall be our endeavour? To bring freedom and opportunity to the common man, to the peasants and workers of India; to fight and end poverty and ignorance and disease; to build up a prosperous, democratic and progressive nation, and to create social, economic and political institutions which will ensure justice and fullness of life to every man and woman.

We have hard work ahead. There is no resting for any one of us till we redeem our pledge in full, till we make all the people of India what destiny intended them to be. We are citizens of a great country on the verge of bold advance, and we have to live up to that high standard. All of us, to whatever religion we may belong, are equally the children of India with equal rights, privileges and obligations. We cannot encourage communalism or narrow-mindedness, for no nation can be great whose people are narrow in thought or in action.

To the nations and peoples of the world we send greetings and pledge ourselves to cooperate with them in furthering peace, freedom and democracy.

And to India, our much-loved motherland, the ancient, the eternal and the ever-new, we pay our reverent homage and we bind ourselves afresh to her service.

JAI HIND [Hail India]

Source: Jawaharlal Nehru, "A Tryst with Destiny," August 14, 1947, "Great Speeches of the 20th Century," *Guardian*, http://www.theguardian.com/theguardian/2007/may/01/greatspeeches.

Source 22.4
Another View of India's Struggle for Independence

Nehru's vision of India as a secular and modernizing state providing a secure home for all of its religious communities was not the only image of the country's struggle for independence. Gandhi was widely viewed as a religious figure, the *mahatma*, or great soul, and the fight against British colonialism, which he led, was often portrayed in distinctly religious and Hindu terms, as Source 22.4, a poster from 1930–1931, illustrates. Here Gandhi is cast as the great Hindu deity Shiva and is portrayed saving a female character representing Mother India from British imperialism, depicted as Yama, the lord of death. This image appropriates the widely known Hindu mythological story of Markandeya, a young and pious sage, who is attacked by Yama, riding a buffalo and seeking to take his soul by casting a rope around the young man. But the great god Shiva rescues Markandeya, grants him eternal life, and slays Yama.

Questions to consider as you examine the source:

■ What features of this legend can you identify in Source 22.4?

■ Why might this image be appealing to Indians in the several decades before independence? To what groups in India might this image raise suspicions or be offensive?

■ How does this image differ from Nehru's depiction of independent India in Source 22.3?

Gandhi and the Fight against British Colonialism

Source 22.5
One Africa

For Kwame Nkrumah, the leader of Ghana's anticolonial movement and the new West African country's first president, independence meant an opportunity to challenge the common assumption that Europe's African colonies should become nation-states within their existing borders. He was convinced that only in a much larger union could the African continent achieve substantial economic development and genuine independence. In doing so, Nkrumah was drawing on the notion of a broader African identity, Pan-Africanism, which had emerged among educated people during the colonial era.

Questions to consider as you examine the source:

■ What kind of union did Nkrumah seek?

■ Why did he think that union was so essential? What benefits would it bring to Africa in its efforts at modern development?

■ What challenges did Nkrumah identify to his soaring vision of a United States of Africa?

KWAME NKRUMAH
Africa Must Unite
1963

There are those who maintain that Africa cannot unite because we lack the three necessary ingredients for unity, a common race, culture, and language. It is true that we have for centuries been divided. The territorial boundaries dividing us were fixed long ago, often quite arbitrarily, by the colonial powers. Some of us are Moslems, some Christians; many believe in traditional, tribal gods. Some of us speak French, some English, some Portuguese, not to mention the millions who speak only one of the hundreds of different African languages. We have acquired cultural differences which affect our outlook and condition our political development. . . .

In the early flush of independence, some of the new African states are jealous of their sovereignty and tend to exaggerate their separatism in a historical period that demands Africa's unity in order that their independence may be safeguarded. . . .

[A] united Africa — that is, the political and economic unification of the African Continent — should seek three objectives: Firstly, we should have an overall economic planning on a continental basis. This would increase the industrial and economic power of Africa. So long as we remain balkanized, regionally or territorially, we shall be at the mercy of colonialism and imperialism. The lesson of the South American Republics vis-à-vis the strength and solidarity of the United States of America is there for all to see.

The resources of Africa can be used to the best advantage and the maximum benefit to all only if they are set within an overall framework of a continentally planned development. An overall economic plan, covering an Africa united on a continental basis, would increase our total industrial and economic power. We should therefore be thinking seriously now of ways and means of building up a Common Market of a United Africa and not allow ourselves to be lured by the dubious advantages of association with the so-called European Common market. . . .

Secondly, we should aim at the establishment of a unified military and defense strategy. . . . For young African States, who are in great need of capital for internal development, it is ridiculous — indeed suicidal — for each State separately and individually to assume such a heavy burden of self-defense, when the weight of this burden could be easily lightened by sharing it among themselves. . . .

The third objective: [I]t will be necessary for us to adopt a unified foreign policy and diplomacy to give political direction to our joint efforts for the protection and economic development of our continent. . . . The burden of separate diplomatic representation by each State on the Continent of Africa alone would be crushing, not to mention representation outside Africa. The desirability of a common foreign policy which will enable us to speak with one voice in the councils of the world, is so obvious, vital and imperative that comment is hardly necessary. . . .

Under a major political union of Africa there could emerge a United Africa, great and powerful, in which the territorial boundaries which are the relics of colonialism will become obsolete and superfluous, working for the complete and total mobilization of the economic planning organization under a unified political direction. The forces that unite us are far greater than the difficulties that divide us at present, and our goal must be the establishment of Africa's dignity, progress, and prosperity.

Source: Kwame Nkrumah, *Africa Must Unite* (London: Heinemann, 1963), 132, 148, 218–21.

Source 22.6
South African "Independence"

Independence in South Africa had a somewhat different meaning than elsewhere in the colonial world, for that country had already ended its colonial relationship with Great Britain in 1910. Thus the struggle in South Africa was against a local entrenched and dominant white minority that had imposed a regime of harsh racial oppression, known as apartheid, that had no parallel in other parts of the world. When that regime ended in April 1994 with the country's first genuinely democratic elections, its demise marked the conclusion of an era in world history in which Europeans exercised formal political control in the African, Asian, Caribbean, and Pacific worlds. This photograph shows a man standing in line preparing to vote in that historic election by displaying his identification document. Such photographs, of which there were thousands, articulated what was for many the essential meaning of that moment.

Questions to consider as you examine the source:

■ Africans had long resented and resisted the requirement to produce on demand an identity card, a kind of internal passport, during the apartheid era. Why, then, do you think that the man in the foreground is proudly displaying his identification document in this photograph?

■ How does the image of several whites, also waiting to vote, enhance the message of the photograph?

■ Notice that the two African men in the foreground are shown in clear focus, while the whites in the background are displayed in a somewhat blurred fashion. Do you think this was deliberate on the part of the photographer? How does this feature of the photo contribute to the message it conveys?

South African Election

© Peter Turnley/Corbis

Source 22.7
Independence as Threat

Independence had meaning not only for those who sought it but also for those who opposed it. In 1961, a Portuguese archbishop in Mozambique, Alvim Pereira, distributed a document to local seminary students and priests that outlined his opposition to independence for Mozambique and other Portuguese colonies.

Questions to consider as you examine the source:

■ How would you summarize the reasons for Alvim Pereira's hostility to independence?

■ What role does the archbishop prescribe for the Catholic Church in confronting independence movements?

■ What kind of future for Mozambique does he imply?

ALVIM PEREIRA
Ten Principles
1961

1. Independence is irrelevant to the welfare of man. It can be good if the right conditions are present (the cultural conditions do not yet exist in Mozambique).

2. While these conditions are not being produced, to take part in movements for independence is acting against nature.

3. Even if these conditions existed, the Metropole has the right to oppose independence if the freedoms and rights of man are respected, and if it [the Metropole] provided for the well-being, for civil and religious progress of all.

4. All the movements which use force (terrorists) are against the natural law. . . .

5. When the movement is a terrorist one, the clergy have the obligation, in good conscience, not only to refrain from taking part but also to oppose it. . . .

6. Even when the movement is peaceful, the clergy must abstain from it in order to have spiritual influence on all people. . . .

7. The native people of Africa have the obligation to thank the colonists for all the benefits which they receive from them.

8. The educated have the duty to lead those with less education from all the illusions of independence.

9. The present independence movements have, almost all of them, the sign of revolt and of Communism; they have no reason. . . .

10. The slogan "Africa for the Africans" is a philosophical monstrosity and a challenge to the Christian civilization, because today's events tell us that it is Communism and Islamism which wish to impose their civilization upon the Africans.

Source: Eduardo Mondlane, *The Struggle for Mozambique* (Penguin Books, 1969), 74–75.

Articulating Independence

1. **Making comparisons:** What do the independence movements described in these sources share? In what ways do they differ?

2. **Defining points of view:** Independence was a widely shared value in the colonial world, but the meanings attached to it varied considerably. How could you use these sources to support this statement?

3. **Imagining a conversation:** Choose three or four of the sources and construct a dialogue between their authors or creators.

Note

1. Todd Shepard, *Voices of Decolonization* (Boston: Bedford/St. Martin's, 2015), 157.

THINKING THROUGH SOURCES

The Future as History

Does the future have a history? Probably not, since what lies ahead is unknown and unknowable, and the discipline of history is relentlessly retrospective. But ideas about the future do have a history. For most of the human journey, ordinary people surely imagined the future as very similar to their present life, for change was slow, almost imperceptible. When ancient cultural or religious figures did imagine a different future, it was often framed as returning to an earlier and better age. Confucius, for example, sought an alternative to the political and social disorder of his time in a return to a former era of imagined tranquility and harmony. Muhammad wanted Jews, Christians, and Arabs alike to return to the primordial religion of Abraham, from which all of them had departed.

With the coming of the Scientific Revolution and the European Enlightenment (see Chapter 15), predictions or imaginations about the future were more often expressed in terms of a sharp break with the past that embodied something altogether new or unprecedented. "The old rubbish must be thrown away," wrote a seventeenth-century English scientist. "These are the days that must lay a new foundation of a more magnificent philosophy."[1] In the nineteenth and early twentieth centuries, followers of Karl Marx and socialists generally looked forward to a future of abundance, equality, and social harmony very different from the sharp class conflicts of rich and poor that characterized all preceding civilizations. And in varying degrees, modern feminists too imagined a radically different future that would put an end to millennia of patriarchy.

The sources that follow present a number of twentieth- and twenty-first-century anticipations, predictions, hopes, and warnings about what lay ahead. The first two sources focus largely on technology from the perspective of early twentieth-century American and European observers. The third conveys something of the aspirations for international life associated with the founding of the United Nations in 1945. In the fourth source, the hopes of the "new nations" released from colonial rule after World War II find expression. These sources invite us to consider the hopes and fears of people living at various times during the last century or so, to assess the accuracy of their forecasts, and in some cases to explain why these visions of the future either came to pass or failed to materialize.

Source 23.1
Looking Ahead from 1900

In December 1900, the *Ladies' Home Journal,* a leading American women's magazine, published an article titled "What May Happen in the Next Hundred Years." It was written by a civil engineer, John E. Watkins, who had worked in the railroad industry and later as a curator for the transportation section of the Smithsonian Museum. He based his predictions on interviews with what he called "the wisest and most careful men in our greatest institutions of science and learning."

Questions to consider as you examine the source:

■ What aspects of life were of special interest to Watkins? What did he neglect or leave out? How might you explain his choice of topics?

■ How would you assess the accuracy of his predictions?

■ How might you describe the overall tone and outlook of Watkins's forecast? How would you explain or account for that point of view?

JOHN E. WATKINS

"What May Happen in the Next Hundred Years"
1900

There will probably be from 350,000,000 to 500,000,000 people in America and its possessions by the lapse of another century. Nicaragua will ask for admission to our Union after the completion of the great canal. Mexico will be next. Europe, seeking more territory to the south of us, will cause many of the South and Central American republics to be voted into the Union by their own people.

The American will be taller by from one to two inches. His increase of stature will result from better health, due to vast reforms in medicine, sanitation, food and athletics. He will live fifty years instead of thirty-five as at present — for he will reside in the suburbs. The city house will practically be no more. Building in blocks will be illegal. The trip from suburban home to office will require a few minutes only. A penny will pay the fare. . . .

There will be no street cars in our large cities. All hurry traffic will be below or high above ground when brought within city limits. . . . These underground or overhead streets will teem with capacious automobile passenger coaches and freight with cushioned wheels. . . . Cities, therefore, will be free from all noises.

Trains will run two miles a minute, normally; express trains one hundred and fifty miles an hour. To go from New York to San Francisco will take a day and a night by fast express. . . .

Automobiles will be cheaper than horses are today. . . . Automobiles will have been substituted for every horse vehicle now known. . . .

There will be air-ships, but they will not successfully compete with surface cars and water vessels for passenger or freight traffic. They will be maintained as deadly war-vessels by all military nations. . . .

[There will be] [a]erial war-ships and forts on wheels. Giant guns will shoot twenty-five miles or more, and will hurl anywhere within such a radius shells exploding and destroying whole cities. . . . These aerial war-ships will necessitate bomb-proof forts, protected by great steel plates over their tops as well as at their sides. . . . Rifles will use silent cartridges. Submarine boats submerged for days will be capable of wiping a whole navy off the face of the deep. . . . Balloons and flying machines will carry telescopes of one-hundred-mile vision with camera attachments, photographing an enemy within that radius. . . .

Photographs will be telegraphed from any distance. If there be a battle in China a hundred years hence snapshots of its most striking events will be published in the newspapers an hour later. . . .

Man will see around the world. Persons and things of all kinds will be brought within focus of cameras connected electrically with screens at opposite ends of circuits, thousands of miles at a span. . . .

Insect screens will be unnecessary. Mosquitoes, house-flies and roaches will have been practically exterminated. . . .

Peas and beans will be as large as beets are to-day. Sugar cane will produce twice as much sugar as the sugar beet now does. . . . Plants will be made proof against disease microbes just as readily as man is to-day against smallpox. The soil will be kept enriched by plants which take their nutrition from the air and give fertility to the earth. . . . Strawberries as large as apples will be eaten by our great-great-grandchildren for their Christmas dinners a hundred years hence. . . . One cantaloupe will supply an entire family. . . .

There will be No C, X or Q in our every-day alphabet. They will be abandoned because unnecessary. Spelling by sound will have been adopted, first by the newspapers. English will be a language of condensed words expressing condensed ideas, and will be more extensively spoken than any other. Russian will rank second. . . .

A university education will be free to every man and woman. . . . Medical inspectors regularly visiting the public schools will furnish poor children free eyeglasses, free dentistry and free medical attention of every kind. The very poor will, when necessary, get free rides to and from school and free lunches between sessions. In vacation time poor children will be taken on trips to various parts of the world. Etiquette and housekeeping will be important studies in the public schools.

Wireless telephone and telegraph circuits will span the world. A husband in the middle of the Atlantic will be able to converse with his wife sitting in her boudoir in Chicago. . . . By an automatic signal they will connect with any circuit in their locality without the intervention of a "hello girl."

Grand Opera will be telephoned to private homes, and will sound as harmonious as though enjoyed from a theatre box. . . . In great cities there will be public opera-houses whose singers and musicians are paid from funds endowed by philanthropists and by the government. . . .

Coal will not be used for heating or cooking. It will be scarce, but not entirely exhausted. The earth's hard coal will last until the year 2050 or 2100; its soft-coal mines until 2200 or 2300. Meanwhile both kinds of coal will have become more and more expensive. Man will have found electricity manufactured by waterpower to be much cheaper. All of our restless waters, fresh and salt, will thus be harnessed to do the work which Niagara is doing today: making electricity for heat, light and fuel.

Hot or cold air will be turned on from spigots to regulate the temperature of a house. . . . Rising early to build the furnace fire will be a task of the olden times.

Pneumatic tubes, instead of store wagons, will deliver packages and bundles . . . and transport mail over certain distances, perhaps for hundreds of miles. . . .

In cold weather he [the farmer] will place heat-conducting electric wires under the soil of his garden and thus warm his growing plants. He will also grow large gardens under glass. At night his vegetables will be bathed in powerful electric light, serving, like sunlight, to hasten their growth. . . .

Fast-flying refrigerators on land and sea will bring delicious fruits from the tropics and southern temperate zone within a few days. The farmers of South America, South Africa, Australia and the South Sea Islands, whose seasons are directly opposite to ours, will thus supply us in winter with fresh summer foods, which cannot be grown here. . . .

Few drugs will be swallowed or taken into the stomach unless needed for the direct treatment of that organ itself. Drugs needed by the lungs, for instance, will be applied directly to those organs through the skin and flesh. They will be carried with the electric current applied without pain to the outside skin of the body. Microscopes will lay bare the vital organs, through the living flesh, of men and animals. The living body will to all medical purposes be transparent. Not only will it be possible for a physician to actually see a living, throbbing heart inside the chest, but he will be able to magnify and photograph any part of it. This work will be done with rays of invisible light. . . .

There will be no wild animals except in menageries. Rats and mice will have been exterminated. . . . Food animals will be bred to expend practically all of their life energy in producing meat, milk, wool and other by-products. . . .

Fast electric ships, crossing the ocean at more than a mile a minute, will go from New York to Liverpool in two days. . . . In storm they will dive below the water and there await fair weather.

Source: John Elfreth Watkins Jr., "What May Happen in the Next Hundred Years," *Ladies' Home Journal*, December 1900, 8.

Source 23.2
Imagining the Future of Technology

Early twentieth-century predictions about the future, at least in the West, focused heavily on technology. A fascinating example of this preoccupation comes from a series of postcards created in 1910 by the French artist Villemard, depicting his vision of life in Paris in the year 2000. Four of the many available images are shown here.

Questions to consider as you examine the sources:

- What aspects of Parisian life does Villemard think will be transformed during the twentieth century? To what extent did his imaginative predictions come to pass?

- To what extent, if at all, are the technological changes matched by changes in gender roles?

- In what ways do these images reflect the sensibility of Watkins's article in Source 23.1?

Source 23.2A
Air Battles and Air Freight in the Future

Un Combat aérien.

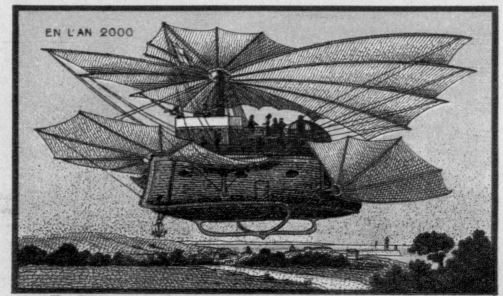

Un Bâtiment des Messageries aériennes.

French color lithograph ca. 1910/Private Collection/Archives Charmet/Bridgeman Images

Source 23.2B
The Horse as a Curiosity

Source 23.2C
The School of the Future

EN L'AN 2000

A l'École.

French chromolithographic educational card, ca. 1910/Private Collection/©Look and Learn/Bridgeman Images

Source 23.2D
A Video–Telephone in the Year 2000

Late-19th-century European chromolithographic educational card/Private Collection/
© Look and Learn/Bridgeman Images

Source 23.3
The United Nations Universal Declaration
of Human Rights

Several months after the end of World War II in 1945, the United Nations
was established in the hope that it could prevent the repetition of any such
horrors. Three years later, the early member states of the UN adopted a
Universal Declaration of Human Rights, the first international expression of such rights. Although none of the member states voted against the
Declaration, a number of them abstained, including the Soviet Union, South
Africa, and Saudi Arabia. Though it is neither legally binding nor enforce-
able, the Declaration has achieved widespread, but not universal, acceptance
as an expression of humankind's highest ideals and has been incorporated
into the constitutions of many countries. Its vision of the future reflected the
sobering experience of two global wars in a single generation and represented
perhaps more of a hope than a prediction.

Questions to consider as you examine the source:

■ Some have argued that the Declaration reflects Western culture and values more than those of other parts of the world. What statements in the Declaration might support this point of view?

■ What parts of the Declaration might have been unacceptable to the Soviet Union, South Africa, and Saudi Arabia?

■ What movements in the direction of the Declaration can you observe in world history since it was adopted? And what violations of its provisions can you identify?

The United Nations Universal Declaration of Human Rights
1948

The General Assembly proclaims this Universal Declaration of Human Rights as a common standard of achievement for all peoples and all nations. . . .

All human beings are born free and equal in dignity and rights. They are endowed with reason and conscience and should act towards one another in a spirit of brotherhood.

Everyone is entitled to all the rights and freedoms set forth in this Declaration, without distinction of any kind, such as race, colour, sex, language, religion, political or other opinion, national or social origin, property, birth or other status.

Furthermore, no distinction shall be made on the basis of the political, jurisdictional or international status of the country or territory to which a person belongs. . . .

Everyone has the right to life, liberty and security of person.

No one shall be held in slavery or servitude; slavery and the slave trade shall be prohibited in all their forms.

No one shall be subjected to torture or to cruel, inhuman or degrading treatment or punishment.

Everyone has the right to recognition everywhere as a person before the law.

All are equal before the law and are entitled without any discrimination to equal protection of the law. . . .

No one shall be subjected to arbitrary arrest, detention or exile. . . .

Everyone charged with a penal offence has the right to be presumed innocent until proved guilty according to law in a public trial at which he has had all the guarantees necessary for his defence. . . .

No one shall be subjected to arbitrary interference with his privacy, family, home or correspondence, nor to attacks upon his honour and reputation. . . .

Everyone has the right to freedom of movement and residence within the borders of each State. Everyone has the right to leave any country, including his own, and to return to his country.

Everyone has the right to seek and to enjoy in other countries asylum from persecution.

Everyone has the right to a nationality. No one shall be arbitrarily deprived of his nationality nor denied the right to change his nationality.

Men and women of full age, without any limitation due to race, nationality or religion, have the right to marry and to found a family. They are entitled to equal rights as to marriage, during marriage and at its dissolution. Marriage shall be entered into only with the free and full consent of the intending spouses.

Everyone has the right to own property alone as well as in association with others. No one shall be arbitrarily deprived of his property.

Everyone has the right to freedom of thought, conscience and religion; this right includes freedom to change his religion or belief, and freedom, either alone or in community with others and in public or private, to manifest his religion or belief in teaching, practice, worship and observance.

Everyone has the right to freedom of opinion and expression; this right includes freedom to hold opinions without interference and to seek, receive and impart information and ideas through any media and regardless of frontiers.

Everyone has the right to freedom of peaceful assembly and association. No one may be compelled to belong to an association.

Everyone has the right to take part in the government of his country, directly or through freely chosen representatives. . . . The will of the people shall be the basis of the authority of government; this will shall be expressed in periodic and genuine elections which shall be by universal and equal suffrage and shall be held by secret vote or by equivalent free voting procedures.

Everyone, as a member of society, has the right to social security and is entitled to realization . . . of the economic, social and cultural rights indispensable for his dignity and the free development of his personality.

Everyone has the right to work, to free choice of employment, to just and favourable conditions of work and to protection against unemployment.

Everyone, without any discrimination, has the right to equal pay for equal work. Everyone who works has the right to just and favourable remuneration ensuring for himself and his family an existence worthy of human dignity, and supplemented, if necessary, by other means of social protection. Everyone has the right to form and to join trade unions for the protection of his interests.

Everyone has the right to rest and leisure, including reasonable limitation of working hours and periodic holidays with pay.

Everyone has the right to a standard of living adequate for the health and well-being of himself and of his family, including food, clothing, housing and medical care and necessary social services, and the right to security in the event of unemployment, sickness, disability, widowhood, old age or other lack of livelihood in circumstances beyond his control. Motherhood and childhood are entitled to special care and assistance. All children, whether born in or out of wedlock, shall enjoy the same social protection.

Everyone has the right to education. Education shall be free, at least in the elementary and fundamental stages. Parents have a prior right to choose the kind of education that shall be given to their children.

Source: From *The Universal Declaration of Human Rights*, General Assembly of the United Nations, adopted December 10, 1948. Reprinted by permission of the United Nations.

Source 23.4
Throwing Off Europe

By the 1960s, independence movements had given birth to dozens of "new nations" all across Africa and Asia. This huge phenomenon was associated with an outpouring of hope for a very different future for these developing countries and for the world. (See Thinking through Sources for Chapter 22.) No one expressed such hopes more extravagantly than Frantz Fanon (1925–1961). Born into a middle-class black family in the French Caribbean island colony of Martinique, Fanon was educated as a psychiatrist in France. In 1953, he found a position in a hospital in Algeria, where he came to identify deeply with the Algerian freedom struggle and more broadly with third-world independence movements in general. In these movements, he found a source of hope for human renewal, but only if colonized people could discard European cultural baggage as well as European political control. Fanon expressed these ideas in his famous book *The Wretched of the Earth,* published in 1961, shortly before his death from leukemia. It was a searing psychological critique of racism and colonialism, which endorsed violence as a potentially liberating experience for colonized people. The book soon gained an international appeal among revolutionary intellectuals in the colonial world and beyond. This excerpt derives from the conclusion to the book.

Questions to consider as you examine the source:

■ Why is Fanon so insistent that newly independent nations should stop imitating Europe? What is he referring to when he urges them to "to stop talking about output, and intensification, and the rhythm of work"?

■ How might you express Fanon's vision of the future? What criticisms might you imagine Fanon's vision of the future provoked? What kinds of people might well be offended by that vision?

■ How do you think Fanon would have responded to the actual evolution of the former colonies since his death?

FRANTZ FANON

The Wretched of the Earth
1961

Come, then, comrades; it would be as well to decide at once to change our ways. We must shake off the heavy darkness in which we were plunged, and leave it behind. The new day which is already at hand must find us firm, prudent and resolute. . . .

Let us waste no time in sterile litanies and nauseating mimicry. Leave this Europe where they are never done talking of Man, yet murder men everywhere they find them, at the corner of every one of their own streets, in all the corners of the globe. For centuries they have stifled almost the whole of humanity. . . . Look at them today swaying between atomic and spiritual disintegration.

Europe has declined all humility and all modesty; but she has also set her face against all solicitude and all tenderness. . . .

So, my brothers, how is it that we do not understand that we have better things to do than to follow that same Europe?

Come, then, comrades, the European game has finally ended; we must find something different. We today can do everything, so long as we do not imitate Europe, so long as we are not obsessed by the desire to catch up with Europe.

Europe now lives at such a mad, reckless pace that she has shaken off all guidance and all reason, and she is running headlong into the abyss; we would do well to avoid it with all possible speed.

Yet it is very true that we need a model, and that we want blueprints and examples. For many among us the European model is the most inspiring. We have therefore seen . . . to what mortifying set-backs such an imitation has led us.

European achievements, European techniques and the European style ought no longer to tempt us and to throw us off our balance.

Two centuries ago, a former European colony decided to catch up with Europe. It succeeded so well that the United States of America became a monster, in which the taints, the sickness and the inhumanity of Europe have grown to appalling dimensions.

Comrades, have we not other work to do than to create a third Europe? . . .

Come, brothers, we have far too much work to do for us to play the game of rear-guard. Europe has done what she set out to do and on the whole she has done it well; let us stop blaming her, but let us say to her firmly that she should not make such a song and dance about it. We have no more to fear; so let us stop envying her.

But let us be clear: what matters is to stop talking about output, and intensification, and the rhythm of work.

No, there is no question of a return to Nature. It is simply a very concrete question of not dragging men towards mutilation, of not imposing upon the brain rhythms which very quickly obliterate it and wreck it. The pretext of catching up must not be used to push man around, to tear him away from himself or from his privacy, to break and kill him.

No, we do not want to catch up with anyone. What we want to do is to go forward all the time, night and day, in the company of Man, in the company of all men. The caravan should not be stretched out, for in that case each line will hardly see those who precede it; and men who no longer recognize each other meet less and less together, and talk to each other less and less.

It is a question of the Third World starting a new history of Man, a history which will have regard to the sometimes prodigious theses which Europe has put forward, but which will also not forget Europe's crimes, of which the most horrible was committed in the heart of man, and consisted of the pathological tearing apart of his functions and the crumbling away of his unity. And in the framework of the collectivity there were the differentiations, the stratification and the bloodthirsty tensions fed by classes; and finally, on the immense scale of humanity, there were racial hatreds, slavery, exploitation and above all the bloodless genocide which consisted in the setting aside of fifteen thousand millions of men.

So, comrades, let us not pay tribute to Europe by creating states, institutions and societies which draw their inspiration from her.

Humanity is waiting for something other from us than such an imitation, which would be almost an obscene caricature.

If we want to turn Africa into a new Europe, and America into a new Europe, then let us leave the destiny of our countries to Europeans. They will know how to do it better than the most gifted among us.

But if we want humanity to advance a step farther, if we want to bring it up to a different level than that which Europe has shown it, then we must invent and we must make discoveries.

If we wish to live up to our peoples' expectations, we must seek the response elsewhere than in Europe.

Moreover, if we wish to reply to the expectations of the people of Europe, it is no good sending them back a reflection, even an ideal reflection, of their society and their thought with which from time to time they feel immeasurably sickened.

For Europe, for ourselves and for humanity, comrades, we must turn over a new leaf, we must work out new concepts, and try to set afoot a new man.

Source: Excerpts from *The Wretched of the Earth*, by Frantz Fanon, English translation copyright © 1963 by Présence Africaine. Used by permission of Grove/Atlantic, Inc. Any third-party use of this material, outside of this publication, is prohibited.

ESSAY QUESTIONS

The Future as History

1. **Using predictions to study the past:** Why might historians be interested in the visions of the futures held by the peoples they study?

2. **Evaluating predictions:** How accurate were the predictions made in 1900, in the 1940s, and in the early 1960s? What twentieth-century developments did these predictions miss altogether? And why?

3. **Comparing perspectives:** Most of these sources reflect the perspectives of people in the Western world. How might predictions about the future from the vantage point of 1900, the 1940s, and 2014 be different if they reflected the concerns of Chinese, Middle Eastern, African, Latin American, Indian, or other peoples of the Global South?

4. **Imagining the future:** How do you imagine the shape of things to come over the next century? Without trying to predict precisely what might happen, can you identify the most important variables that will affect the future? To what extent will conscious human actions contribute to that future?

Note

1. Quoted in Steven Shapin, *The Scientific Revolution* (Chicago: University of Chicago Press, 1996), 66.